To Beth
from Daniel, Diane, Nilo
and Britta   April 1980

A Picture History of Alberta

TONY CASHMAN

HURTIG PUBLISHERS
Edmonton

Hurtig Publishers
10560 – 105 Street
Edmonton, Alberta

Design: Brant Cowie/Artplus Ltd.

CANADIAN CATALOGUING IN PUBLICATION DATA
Cashman, Tony, 1923–
  A picture history of Alberta

  ISBN 0-88830-157-X

  1. Alberta — History — Pictorial works.
I. Title.
FC3661.C38   971.230022'2
C78-002108-8   F1078.C38

Printed and bound in Canada

Introduction

THE HISTORY OF ALBERTA has been conducted almost entirely under camera surveillance, in vivid contrast with older places. In Ireland, once upon a time, my wife Veva and I made inquiries about a ruined tower that stood stark and lonely on a fierce granite headland battered day and night by black Atlantic swells. We were assured that the ruin was of no historical significance "as it dates from 1450 is all." Except for the Indians of prehistory and the fur traders of the Hudson's Bay Company empire, the activities of all Albertans have been documented by the camera.

The camera enjoys a reputation of shining incorruptibility quite undeserved, since it can cheat, distort, and deceive, though often in so good a cause as civic pride. Pioneer photographers liked to shoot street scenes on parade days to make their town seem the bustling metropolis its boosters intended to make it. On the other hand the camera can often stab to the heart of a truth, as it did in the hands of Randolph Bruce in 1893 when it recorded the expression of a lone Indian standing outside a white man's fence, an outsider in his own country.

In a conventional history built of words, political leaders and their speeches and letters tend to dominate. But in the eye of the camera, political figures shrink to the stature of ordinary people and often seem less relevant. Could that be a truth the camera wants to convey? Since this is a photographic history, it tells the story the camera tells best — and that should occasion neither surprise nor apology.

A statistician asked for a history of Alberta will produce a chronicle containing only those truths that can be expressed in columns of figures. The folk singer, from Homer to Gordon Lightfoot, has related only that part of history suitable for song. When Jack Weaver the sculptor is commissioned to portray Alberta history, he selects those forces and emotions in the story that result in the best sculpture. When Rick Grandmaison was asked by TransCanada Pipelines to portray the start of ranching in Alberta, he selected a highlight to provide an effective canvas.

So a photo history, though limited like any other, has strengths like no other if the strange powers of the camera are recognized. The camera has great story-telling power, but this power diminishes and totally disappears as the camera comes close to something we know and see every day.

A picture of modern-day traffic on the High Level Bridge — however artful — can add little further to an Edmontonian's understanding of that subject. But if he could see a picture of a car parked in the middle of the bridge in 1913 so that two girls might go to the rail and gaze into the awful abyss and then pose smiling in front of their parked car — if he could see that picture, he would receive at a glance a story of 1913 traffic and the year 1913 in general. That picture is in this book.

Almost every owner of a car has experienced the Calgary-Edmonton highway — six lanes of concrete with a grass divider. No photograph, however artful, can add much to his understanding of that road. But if he could journey back to 1906 and stand beside J. H. Gano on a hill near Wainwright and photograph two meandering ruts — the only marks of mankind on a huge landscape — which four settlers' wagons are following to their promised homestead, he would gain appreciation of all highways. That picture is in this book too.

The truly informative picture becomes scarce after 1950. Proximity to the present is one problem; immensity is another. In 1902 a cameraman backed off one hundred feet and imprinted on his glass plate the entire drilling site of Alberta's first producing oil well, wooden derrick and all. In 1977 Ken Orr was able to get the Syncrude site in one frame by backing off half a mile horizontally and half a mile vertically in a helicopter.

Immensity may be overcome with a helicopter, but there is the further problem of complexity. Consider the origin of the Viking gas field. The photographer has caught it all in just one frame. It's 1914. The president of the Edmonton Industrial Association is starting the first well — with a shovel. Ranged behind him are confident boosters who have subscribed a hundred dollars apiece so that their favourite city may have the advantage of natural gas. In contrast, the origins of the Syncrude project are so complex and so subtle as to baffle the mind, let alone an instrument which can record only the surface indicators of primary forces. A visual study of Syncrude's beginnings would become a text with a supporting cast of pictures and cease to be a picture history.

The camera began to lose some of its grip on history at about the point where television was developed, and, although the timing was coincidental, an important point has evolved. Television puts the world in a box, a square box that allows no choice of proportion with regard to breadth or height. The view of the classic photographer was in a proportion of five to seven, seven wide or seven tall, according to his artistic judgment of which served better to showcase the subject. Since there was rarely anything high to shoot at, he nearly always took the broad view and often surrounded the subject with wide open spaces. To practical people who tacked pictures into wooden frames, these spaces appeared to be blanks, to be trimmed like excess fat in a butcher shop. But these were the wide open spaces which challenged the minds of Victorians and Edwardians, an essential part of the story the photographer wanted the camera to tell.

A classic "space shot" rarely seen in its entirety is W.J. Oliver's study of the 15th Alberta Light Horse, a cavalry troop drawn up in smart parade order on the dusty plain of Sarcee. The 15th was organized in 1906 by a Calgary alderman to perpetuate the cavalry tradition founded by western riders in the South African War, and it contained squadrons from Calgary, Cochrane, High River, and Innisfail. Oliver moved back from the formation so that there might be space to the left of them, space to the right of them. He then moved up an incline so that the eye of the camera could sweep down the slope of spiky grass and pursue each detail of horseman's landscape, wider and wider to all horizons. Oliver's uncut original showed not only the 15th Alberta Light Horse, but, without a word of explanation, why Alberta had a cavalry tradition before the First World War and sent four mounted units into that conflict. A picture which demands a thousand words to be understood makes a mockery of the ancient Chinese proverb and has the impact of a joke that needs explaining.

In the pages that follow there are some four hundred photographs which can speak for themselves after a brief introduction. They are the work of skilled professionals who left little to chance and amateurs who, by happy chance, opened their shutters on important truths. With noted exceptions, they were found in the rich archives of the Glenbow-Alberta Institute in Calgary.

In defining a format for this book it was decided that there should be no separation of photo and text. In fact, that there should be no text as such, but a progression of pictures bound by interlocking captions. Then came the question of arrangement. Should they be arranged chronologically or by subject? Both have advantages. Very well then, let us have both.

Subjects are introduced in chronological order and are carried forward to some logical termination or interval, then the scanner moves back to bring in the next subject. A subject may be a group of people — the surveyors; an individual — the Marquis of Lorne; a movement — the Women Are People campaign of 1916-1929; or a feeling — the booster euphoria which levitated the new cities of Alberta from 1905 to 1914.

The parade order is published on the following page.

Contents

The Fur Traders

THE CAMERA CAME TOO LATE to record the golden age of the fur trade empire. Fortunately, Toronto artist Paul Kane passed this way in 1846 and '47 when the dominance of the Hudson's Bay Company was at its zenith. Paul Kane's paintings are not literal reproductions of reality — he invests all he sees with the romantic Victorianism that caused him to make the journey in the first place. Indian ponies tend to become Arabians, and clumsy York boats treasure galleons of a classic past. But his impression of Edmonton in late September 1846 is confirmed by photographs a generation later.

"Edmonton is a large establishment ..." he writes. "There are usually here a chief factor and a clerk, with forty or fifty men with their wives and children, amounting altogether to about 130, who all live within the pickets of the fort."

Kane's view is from the site of today's city power plant. He's facing up the hill that the first government of Alberta will choose for the domed legislative building. He's drawing the fourth Fort Edmonton, built in 1821 with the merger of rival trading companies. Although a fort, it's made of soft local wood, the same wood of which eight hundred cords a year are burned in the forges and fireplaces. The river is the highway to the outside world. In spring the boat brigade goes down to Hudson Bay with the winter's accumulation of fur and returns with supplies for another year of trading.

Kane writes of "A Buffalo Pound": "During the whole of the three days it took us to reach Edmonton House we saw nothing else but these animals covering these plains as far as the eye could reach, and so numerous were they that at times they impeded our progress, filling the air with dust almost to suffocation." In the picture the Indians are herding the buffalo into a pound which then becomes a slaughter house. In the Northwest Rebellion of 1885, Louis Riel's general, Gabriel Dumont, will use the tactic of the buffalo pound to delay the advance of a larger army.

At one stop in his "Wanderings of an Artist," Kane paints the Medicine Pipe Dance, a Blackfoot religious ceremony. The fur traders have no forts in the territory of the Blackfoot who are unimpressed by the Royal Charter. The traders prefer the wooded parkland of the North Saskatchewan valley and the company of the easy-going Crees. The Blackfoot dance is a prayer to the Spirit of the Thunder. The medicine pipe is richly carved and entrusted to one person who keeps it bundled in sacred cloths until brought forth for the ceremony. The dance is performed in early summer, at the first manifestation of the Thunder Spirit, or at other times to draw strength from the Spirit when embarking on a journey or hunt.

After a year of artistic wandering through the mountains, Kane spends Christmas of 1847 at Fort Edmonton. There is feasting and dancing, and the dance leads to the earliest portrait of a resident of Edmonton.

"Another lady with whom I sported the light fantastic toe, whose poetic name was Cun-ne-wa-bum, or 'One that looks at the Stars,' was a half-breed Cree girl; and I was so much struck by her beauty that I prevailed upon her to sit for her likeness, which she afterwards did with great patience, holding her fan, which was made of the tip end of swan's wing with an ornamental handle of porcupine's quills."

The coloured glass beads in Cun-ne-wa-bum's costume are the best-known item of trade between whites and Indians. They spare native women the arduous task of slicing and dyeing porcupine quills.

But there's more to the fur trade than beads. Many items of trade are preserved in Fort Edmonton Historical Park and show why Cun-ne-wa-bum's people welcomed the arrangement. To a people using the weapons of the Stone Age, the Hudson's Bay Company brings simultaneously the Bronze Age and the Iron Age. What could be more logical than tomahawks made in Birmingham, England?

The native tomahawk has a head of chipped stone. The British import combines two ages of metallurgy in one instrument: a brass head with an inset cutting edge of iron.

Tomahawks are popular, but the most sought-after items are domestic utensils:

Copper kettles, in two styles, with copper handles so that they can be hung over a campfire.

Pewter dishes. The device inscribed at the top has not been identified but is likely an equivalent of Baycrest.

Iron forks, with handles of bone or oak.

And an all-purpose knife of crude steel known as the Green River knife because it's been developed in Green River, Massachusetts. The wily fur traders have it copied by the same foundries that supply tomahawks.

The Missionaries

THE FUR TRADERS have been the first outside group to exert an influence on Alberta. The next group, much smaller, has an influence beyond mere numbers. In the 1840s the missionaries begin arriving. Admirers have built up legends about the missionaries. Well meant, the legends tend nevertheless to obscure their achievements. The camera dispels some wrong impressions.

This is the enduring image that a well-meaning artist created for Robert Rundle, first of his fraternity in Alberta, who served the Methodist Church from 1840 to '48. From a photograph of Rundle in old age, the artist conjured up a large, whiskery prophet out of the Old Testament, laying down the law of God with fire and brimstone.

But here is the real Robert Rundle after his return to England and marriage to Mary Wolverson. In the 1850s the camera records a slight and frail Victorian gentleman beside a wisp of a lady who might have caused Charles Dickens to invent Little Dorrit. From a source beyond understanding, this delicate man found the strength to journey to the Rocky Mountains and to enter them as far as Banff. His health broke and he went home and never returned, but Robert Rundle was still living when Canada named a mountain in honour of his mission to Banff.

A Victorian would likely remember it with mist off the eternal snows shrouding its base.

Admirers of George McDougall liked to think of him as a man of granite visage, patterned on prophets of the Old Testament. This retouched photograph shows the cherished image.

But the real George McDougall looks far less certain of himself and surprisingly vulnerable — which he was. In January 1876, aged fifty-four, he froze to death travelling alone in a snowstorm from Calgary to the Methodist mission at Morley.

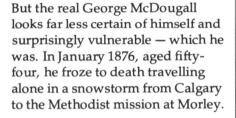

John McDougall, George's son, was a missionary too and wrote popular adventure books based on travels with his father and other churchmen. *Saddle, Sled and Showshoe* and *Forest, Lake and Prairie* recount day-to-day hardships of the life, including the diet. As a youth he sickened on the eternal salt meat and pemmican. A passage in the book describes his longing for a taste of bread.

This building is now the oldest in Edmonton, McDougall's mission church of 1871. Inside a protective shell, it stood almost on its original location, less than a block from Jasper and 101st Street, until 1978 when it was moved to Fort Edmonton Park.

Father Lacombe's historic image is based on his appearance in old age, in particular at this famous 1909 garden party where he reminisces with Lord Strathcona and, having commiserated with the Scottish-born empire builder on an arm broken while riding, suggests that Strathcona might like to give him a souvenir for his orphans (a cheque will arrive the next day).

In the vigour of his long youth Father Lacombe stood erect and wiry, strong-featured and, on occasion, strong-tempered. In his fifties he visits Ottawa with Blackfoot chiefs Crowfoot and Three Bulls.

This sketch by Father Emile Petitot shows the mission at St. Albert, founded by Father Lacombe in 1863, the beginning of a community that became Alberta's tenth city in 1977. The church, like McDougall's mission, is now in a protective shell.

From 1886 to '89, Charles Gordon lived in this house at Banff and rode through the mountains for the Presbyterian church. His adventures in mining camps and ranch houses start him on a writing career of twenty-nine books. This is the third, published in 1899 under the Reverend Charles Gordon's famous pen name of Ralph Connor.

In the golden sunlight of Queen Victoria's reign, adventurous young Englishmen prize a period of service in the outposts of Empire. Quite the proper thing. The Church of England expects every man to do his duty with three years in the mission fields. Standards are maintained of course. In 1892 Mr. Haynes with Victorian wife and Victorian baby pose as for an English garden party in the bare yard of their home on the Piegan Reserve near Fort Macleod.

At the turn of the century the main mission field is in the densely wooded foothills west of Edmonton. In correct attire of the frontiersman, Mr. Ball relaxes beside his sod-roofed cabin at Greencourt.

The Steinhauer Saga

Henry Bird Steinhauer was born Shawahnekezhik, about 1818, on an Ojibway reserve in Ontario. He was sponsored for a Methodist seminary in Pennsylvania by a Philadelphia banker named Steinhauer whose son had died. Shawahnekezhik took the name of his sponsor's late son. He was sent to the West by the church. In 1855 he founded a mission at Whitefish Lake, now in eastern Alberta. In his busy life he found time to translate into Cree the entire New Testament and many books of the Old.

Henry Bird Steinhauer had a large family. Two sons, Egerton and Robert, were ordained ministers. Robert is thought to be the first native to earn a B.A. and be awarded an honorary Doctorate of Divinity. Another son Arthur (1852-1929) was a farmer and carpenter at church missions. Arthur had a son James Arthur (1883-1969).

In 1907 James Arthur was stationed here at the Morley Reserve when the blacksmith Josia Apow died, leaving a widow and a son a year old. James Arthur married Mrs. Apow and adopted the little boy, who grew up as Ralph Steinhauer. Ralph became a farmer at Saddle Lake and a leader in farm organizations.

In the spring of 1974 Ralph and his American-born wife Isabel stroll through the flakes of a late snow in front of the house where he has heard that he is to be Alberta's tenth lieutenant-governor.

North West Mounted Police

ON JULY 15TH, 1870, the fur trade empire of the Hudson's Bay Company passes to the Dominion of Canada. After two hundred years, the Company surrenders all its rights under the royal charter for fifteen million dollars and a thousand acres around each trading post. Canada has acquired "a great lone land," as Captain Butler wrote. Canada must express a presence there.

To Manitoba the fledgling country has sent a raw, undisciplined militia bent on hanging the rebel Louis Riel and harassing his supporters, a public relations disaster which is not repeated as Canada looks farther west. To the Northwest Territories, extending beyond Manitoba to the Rocky Mountains, the country decides to send a professional police cavalry on a mission more subtle and complex than merely enforcing the law. It's expressed in their motto, *Maintiens le droit* — Maintain the right. Recruits respond to ads like this in newspapers of Ontario.

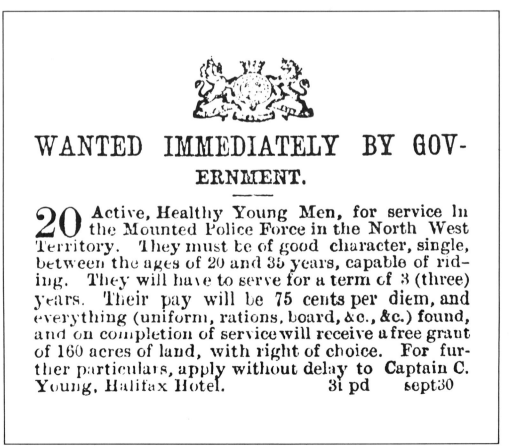

WANTED IMMEDIATELY BY GOV-
ERNMENT.

20 Active, Healthy Young Men, for service in the Mounted Police Force in the North West Territory. They must be of good character, single, between the ages of 20 and 35 years, capable of riding. They will have to serve for a term of 3 (three) years. Their pay will be 75 cents per diem, and everything (uniform, rations, board, &c., &c.) found, and on completion of service will receive a free grant of 160 acres of land, with right of choice. For further particulars, apply without delay to Captain C. Young, Halifax Hotel.   3i pd   sept30

In the summer of 1874 the North West Mounted Police make the long trek across the prairies. With them is artist Henri Julien, only twenty years old, about the age of most recruits, and just beginning to develop the style that will make him Canada's most renowned political cartoonist. There is little grass for the horses and the domestic farm animals that the Mounties are taking to promote agriculture. Here the party has come in sight of the Sweetgrass Hills where good forage is promised.

Mounted Police forts mark the sites of permanent communities to come. They found Fort Macleod and Fort Saskatchewan, and in picking a location for Fort Calgary they certainly have all the country to choose from. The camera (1878) is pointed northwest with the Elbow River in the foreground.

Ending the whisky trade is the first priority of the new force. Police surgeon Dr. R. B. Nevitt sketches the trial of a whisky trader. The scene is a famous frontier store, Spitzee Post on the Highwood River, run by "Liver-Eating" Johnston. The counter becomes the bar of justice. The magistrate makes notes as an Indian testifies through an interpreter. One policeman acts as prosecutor while another, facing us, acts as court orderly.

The work of maintaining the right involves many people. These are some of the key men at Fort Macleod. The middle row are regular members of the Force: Inspector Cecil Denny, Staff Sergeant Hilliard, and Sergeant Cotter. Elk-Facing-The-Wind and Black Eagle are scouts from the Blood Indian reserve. Two other scouts stand behind: Mr. Hunbury and the storied Métis, Jerry Potts.

A major problem for the Force is communication over the wide spaces. On April 5th, 1879, dispatch rider James Schofield poses for the tintype photographer at Fort Calgary. In 1894 the Mounties arrange the building of the first long-distance telephone line in Alberta — Lethbridge to the U.S. border.

In addition to law and order, the Mounties bring settlement. Most serve five years and pick a spot to settle for themselves. They also bring the music of the military band to augment the native drums and pipes and the fiddles of the traders. The Musical Ride, sketched by Frederick Remington, needs a band.

The bands play for all occasions. In 1886 the H Troop Band performs at a church picnic in Lethbridge.

The bands play for fancy balls, of which there are none in the whole Territories fancier than those arranged by the men of the Force. Here is a period piece composed by the father of Inspector Crozier, an important figure in the Northwest Rebellion of 1885. The cover features the founder of Fort Macleod and an artist's impression of the land in which the Mounted Police *maintiens le droit.*

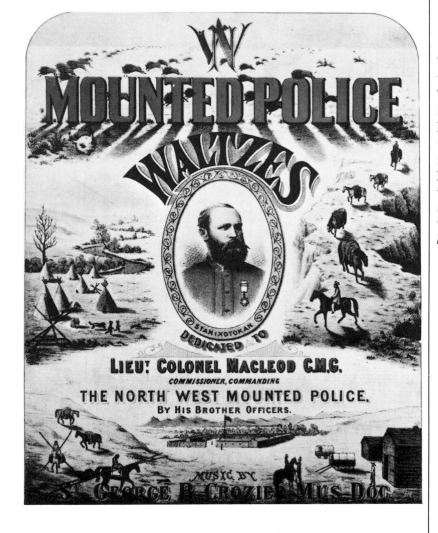

The Surveyors

AFTER THE MOUNTED POLICE come the surveyors. The great lone land is unmarked and undivided. The land has been held in common by the natives and fur traders, but now it must be marked in squares for individuals — rugged individuals who will come to claim title to their part of it and invest that portion with their toil and hopes.

Here is the approach of a typical crew, surveying the boundaries of future farms in southern Alberta. This is CPR land, land which the railroads receive in vast blocks to help finance construction.

The surveyors mark the 49th Parallel with sod pyramids... then strike off on lines running true north and true west, marking each mile of their progress with an iron stake.

Here is a surveyor's wagon, a moving dot on a sea of grass, working into the Crowsnest Pass. Turtle Mountain shows hazily in the middle distance in the left, the mountain that will collapse on the town of Frank.

On the open grassland of the south the surveyors can travel on wheels, but in the wooded and gullied north pack animals are needed and the job of packing the stove goes to the horse of most serene temper, the horse least likely to wander off into the woods with the camp kitchen. This stove horse is named Wanbee. The name of the cook is not recorded.

Rivers and streams make a complete reversal of character. In the fur-trade past David Thompson and Peter Fidler charted them as routes of commerce. But in the New West rivers are barriers to everyone including surveyors. Fording is one way to cross.

When poling a hand-made raft, getting there is half the fun.

A surveyor's life was not all work, nor were all the stakes driven into the ground. In 1890 a party marking the route of the Calgary-Edmonton railway relaxes over a card game.

In 1911 another party brings the culture of a rhythm band to the Peace River Country.

One of the legendary figures of this rugged breed is Andrew McVittie, who arrived from Ontario in 1883 in time to participate in the record season of twenty-seven million acres surveyed. McVittie's credits include the townsites of Fort Macleod and Calgary. Seen here in 1883, he stands at the far right, gazing appropriately into the distance.

Directly behind McVittie is his house, fashioned from packing crates and from driftwood logs found in the Bow River. Believed to be the oldest house from the townsite, McVittie's house rests today in Heritage Park, Calgary.

The men with the transits, rods, and sixty-six-foot chains are genuine folk heroes. Sailor suit to the contrary, Master Bowden Lunn of Langdon shows that he wants to be a surveyor when he grows up. Although it's 1914, Master Lunn has lots of time. The survey is still going on.

The Marquis of Lorne

IN THE SUMMER OF 1881 the governor general of Canada crosses the prairies. Thirty-six years old and fired by the soaring imagination of the Victorian age, the Marquis of Lorne rides the Canadian Pacific Railway to the end of steel at Portage la Prairie. Then he leaves the railroad and the province of Manitoba, and sets off by wagon to see the Northwest Territories, urging all within range of his enthusiasm to be awed and uplifted by the prospects of the country. His own keen-eyed appreciation is poured into sketches — which are good enough for the *Illustrated London News,* the prestige pictorial of the age.

In late August the governor's party crosses the Red Deer River, about thirty miles downstream from the present city of Red Deer. He pauses to sketch the soft bluffs that weather into hoodoos farther down the river.

He goes to Blackfoot Crossing to meet the chiefs who signed historic Treaty Number Seven only four years earlier. He draws the impressive setting and the wagons waiting to meet him.

Approaching Calgary from the northeast, he comes out on heights overlooking the Bow River and orders a sketching stop. Even the most travelled of visitors are unprepared for the massive wall of the Rocky Mountains. "What a possession to Canada these glorious Alps!" writes the Reverend James MacGregor of Edinburgh, reporting on the vice-regal tour for the *Scotsman.* Says MacGregor, "No wonder Lord Lorne paused to sketch one of the most beautiful scenes of the beautiful land he governs. Behind us lay the yellow prairie stretching as far as the eye could see. On the south horizon rose a mighty pillar of cloud like that which guided Israel.... Due southwest we looked straight on the great range, whose base was now only forty-five miles away."

The governor general sees a dramatic expanse of unbroken country with majestic mountains for a backdrop. And he foresees something as well. Take any section of the picture, add a cross of St. George at the top and a stand of grain in the foreground field, and you have the crest of the Province of Alberta, which will be adopted a quarter century into the future.

It's the vision of a true Victorian, and if any man may be called such it must be the Marquis of Lorne, whose wife is the fourth daughter of the Queen herself.

Here she is dressed for a drive. A liberated woman, she declined to be married off to a European prince as her older sisters had been, deciding that she would marry a Briton even if it did mean going outside the ranks of royalty as no princess had done for three hundred years. She chose the marquis, who, though he was heir to the dukedom of Argyll, was a subject and, worse, a political follower of Mr. Gladstone, no friend of the Queen.

On his tour of the Northwest Territories, the romantic Victorian proposes creating a province which he can name for his princess — Louise Caroline Alberta. The Territories he sketches with such interest are not ready for province-hood, but the likable Scot is so persuasive that the following year the government agrees to name a district of the Northwest Territories after the princess. Already there are three districts in the prairies: Assiniboia, Saskatchewan, and Athabasca (named for the three great river systems). By rearranging the boundaries, a fourth is added — Alberta. If it weren't for the marquis, the province would almost certainly be known today as Athabasca.

And the Canadian Pacific Railway has a further honour to confer on the popular princess. The most beautiful lake in Alberta is given her first name.

The Railroad Builders

IN 1883 THE RAILROAD BUILDERS enter Alberta on their westward drive. The first major obstacle is the South Saskatchewan River at Medicine Hat. Their bridge is photographed by a man from the Notman Studio of Montreal. Although the scene looks peaceful, this is the spring of 1885. The Riel Rebellion is underway, and the larger boat under the bridge, the *Northcote*, will soon be converted to a warship to attack Riel's river stronghold of Batoche.

Every Monday the Canadian Pacific runs colonist trains from Montreal and Toronto, bringing people to the New West. On the platform of the Medicine Hat station a crowd watches the return of the eastbound express pulled by the well-known Engine 98.

Eastbound freights tend to rattle empty as the new country gets slowly into production.

But, for a brief period, relics of the Old West offer a cash crop to settlers and cargo to the CPR. As buffalo chips once fertilized the prairies, the bones are now gathered and ground up to fertilize the gardens of the East. This impressive build-up is shot near Medicine Hat in 1884. It is a very selective pile built of buffalo skulls only.

By the end of the century the railroad builders will have laid a thousand miles of track on the face of Alberta. Branching off from Calgary, they move south through the Crowsnest Pass and north to Edmonton. Each hard-won mile is earned with physical exertion. This gang is working toward Edmonton in 1890, and the prospect is exciting for travellers. They'll be able to make the journey from Calgary in eighteen hours, some improvement over five days on the stagecoach.

In 1898 a young Scot comes to the Calgary ticket office, planning to head north and start a newspaper. He has just enough money to buy a ticket to siding number sixteen. He knows there'll be a town there. This is the town — it's Wetaskiwin.

Here is the young Scot — it's Bob Edwards in his days of later fame as editor of the Calgary *Eye Opener*.

Faces of the New West

FACES OF THE NEW WEST express confidence in the prospects of the country and greater confidence in themselves. No self-doubt assails these fine fellows gathered for sport on a foothills ranch. They have renounced the strictures (and the comforts) of old societies and found on the frontier a rugged-and-ready liberty, equality, and fraternity.

In Calgary a frame hut with a canvas roof offers all the security required by Mr. and Mrs. John Birchall and daughter Hilda.

In 1886 at Fort Macleod some occasion brings together Thomas William Ireland, his family, and his friends. Mr. Ireland, with the bottle, appears ready to propose a toast to good companions. Mr. Ireland's interest in the bottle transcends mere consumerism, however. He will found the first brewery in Medicine Hat.

Frederick Remington draws the shoppers in a Hudson's Bay Company store.

There are Indians in Remington's picture, but for Wolf Head and his son, seen at Gleichen in the 1880s, there is no real place in the New West of confident whites.

Wolf Head and son are better off than they would be in the United States, as cartoonist John Innes tries to show in this magazine cover. The Canadian native can have theology, rhetoric, simple equations, and the writings of humorist Bill Nye, while all an Indian can expect from Uncle Sam is a punch in the snoot.

There is truth in the cartoon, but the greater truth is that the Indian has become an outsider in his own land. A desolation of spirit comes over him and lasts nearly a hundred years. Photographer Randolph Bruce seems to have captured it all. It's 1893 or '94. A Blackfoot stands outside a white man's fence and gazes off into a distance in which there is no horizon.

The Ranchers

IN THE FIRST WAVE of new faces ranch people dominate. Big ranching gets a big start — here recalled in a dramatic painting done by Rick Grandmaison and commissioned by TransCanada Pipelines for the Calgary centennial. In 1881 thousands of cattle are driven from Montana to the open range near present-day Cochrane.

Cattle

Maj. Walkers estimate of Stock
as at Apl. 1st 1882.

Cows	3330
Heifer Calves	705
" Yearlings	692
Steers. 3 yoo.	523 }
2 "	788 }
1 "	693
Bull Calves	705
Durham Bulls	5
Hereford "	41
Polled Angus -	9
Grade -	138
Work Oxen.	10
	7639
add	212
	7,851
deduct	597
Approximate number on hand.	7.254

The visionary financier behind the risky venture is Quebec business-man and senator Matthew Henry Cochrane (left).

Can cattle survive on the open range so far north? The crucial first winter passes. In April 1882 the manager of the ranch makes a count of the herds. Success is obvious; others will follow. The manager is Major Walker, former Mounted Police-man. In the same celebration that occasions the Grandmaison paint-ing, James Walker will be named Calgary's citizen of the century.

In time, the senator's son Billy makes his own mark as historic trend-setter. In 1901 Billy Cochrane brings the first motor vehicle into Alberta, this steam-powered Locomobile with the wicker basket for stowing parasols. One motor vehicle among seventy-three thousand people is 0.0000137 per capita. In 1977, with a population of almost two million, Alberta will have virtually 0.8 per capita, among the highest in North America.

The life of the North American cow-boy is celebrated in story and song. Here's an apt illustration for any song or any story. It's about 1900. The cowboys take their positions for the start of a roundup near Cochrane. They'll be rounding up those critters in the background and hundreds more out of the camera's view.

The very model of the ranch home where seldom is heard a discouraging word. This picturesque scene is the setting for the home of J. A. W. Fraser of Little Jumping Pound. It's the sort of spread Robert J. C. Stead writes about.

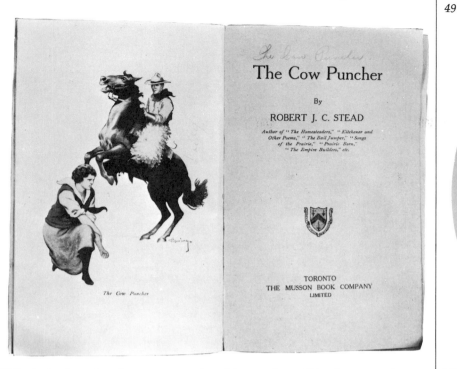

The Cow Puncher

You'll find Mr. Stead in the immigration department of the CPR in Calgary. Dynamic salesman-publicity man, he pours out reams of rose-hued prose extolling the clean, healthy vigour of life in the open spaces — spaces opened courtesy of the CPR and available at good prices. On his own time, Mr. Stead writes in the same vein — poetry too in the spirit of Walt Whitman — and becomes one of Canada's best-known authors. Here are the title page and frontispiece of a popular novel derived from his travels among Alberta ranch people.

Horses do well in the open. Imported breeding stock thrive as well on the range as the wild Indian ponies that worked their way into the Alberta foothills from the south late in the eighteenth century. A growing population creates a growing demand for horses — for work on farms, in mines, and for making deliveries in urban centres. By 1920 the horse population hits a high, outnumbering the people eight hundred thousand to six hundred thousand.

These horses are from the J.J. Bowlen ranch at Rosebud. Each spring, J.J. sets off along the new railroad lines in Saskatchewan, selling workhorses. Here he has arrived at Humboldt. J.J. Bowlen is the big man mounted left of centre.
In 1950 he will become Alberta's Vice-Regal Cowboy, lieutenant-governor number seven.

Compared to horses, sheep aren't much as rodeo performers, though young Percy Copithorne finds this one an exciting enough mount. Percy's ride is recorded at Jumping Pound in 1904, the year after the devastating spring blizzard that hit the southern ranges at lambing time, killing most of the young sheep.

This scene on the hills near Cardston is peaceful. But clement weather, on which the life of the open range depends, is ever subject to cancellation without notice.

This is a spring scene near Beynon following the terrible winter of 1906-07 in which thirty percent of range stock perished. The winter has passed, but the cow has died of exhaustion and the calf faces an uncertain future.

Over the long years, Alberta shows progress in many things, but the weather remains stubbornly undependable. The blizzard that has let the cows jump over the roof of this farmhouse, at Elnora, has come in 1950.

The Homesteaders

MANY PROBLEMS BESET the cattle, horse, and sheep ranchers who graze their stock on leased, open ranges. They can fight disease, treacherous weather, and treacherous markets, but here comes the problem that finally defeats them. These are settlers moving toward their personal promised land — 160 acres each — along two ruts, the only marks of occupation on this Wainwright-area landscape of 1906. They're all called homesteaders though some buy land outright from the railroads while others enter under the Homestead Act and gain title by building a house and breaking thirty acres a year.

Clearing and breaking are heavier going in the wooded parkland of the north. It's 1911 near Edson. Finlay Maxwell and his family are so pleased with what they've accomplished in five months that they have summoned a cameraman to bear witness.

Meeting the requirements for a title is easier in the open where nature has done the clearing and two walking ploughs can make silhouettes on the big sky. This is Roy Benson's place near Munson in 1910. The ploughs have already broken the plain to make a fireguard.

A frame house is the dream home of the settler, though this one on the former range of the Bow River Horse Ranch is more of a nightmare to the ranchers.

Here is a dream interior — John Beam's house north of Cochrane, where a family can gather round the oil lamp in all kinds of weather.

A frame house is the ideal, but a settler can find material for a beginning shelter right on his claim. Fresh-cut sods from the virgin prairie make neat building blocks.

In the region of Haneyville (about 1907) sods have provided a house and a connecting barn.

A tornado has hit McLaughlin (about 1912) and blown away the roof and tumbled the chimney of the Bull mansion, but the walls have held firm. The wind has not made off with Mrs. Bull's best hat nor the table made of a crate of Force, a popular breakfast cereal.

If the passengers will look behind them they can see one of the sights, a sod church, Castor's first.

Our First Homestead

A nearby stand of trees has provided *Our First Homestead* (1902-05) for the Summers family, settlers from Nebraska in the Erskine district.

Tom Ogden of Bingley achieves architectural flair with logs, vertical and horizontal.

Milt Hickey of Cremona has added touches of permanent class, a shingle roof and a hand-whittled porte-cochère. It's the winter of 1896, and Milt's friend Hugh Anderson has ridden Calico through the snow for a visit.

A shack built of finished lumber has this advantage. On smooth walls the homesteader's equipment can be hung in neat array. On a fine day in the Wainwright district this bachelor "lets it all hang out."

Tar paper makes good insulation. Homer Houghton can laugh at the rude winds that blow over Claresholm. That's Homer standing by the corner of the house to welcome his visitors.

This is a dugout sunk two steps into the ground to give the elements less to batter. It's the home of Rufus Belt of the Stettler district — or was. Belt was murdered and robbed here by an overnight guest, a crime that outraged pioneers everywhere and made the capture of the killer a sensational headline on January 25th, 1904. Ernest Cashel was hanged without regret. He had committed murder. He had also violated the code of hospitality on which the pioneer community depended for life.

Growth of Government

THE NATIONAL GOVERNMENT mounts an international campaign to attract settlers. High-pressure salesmen, vivid posters, and a magazine called *The Last Best West* circulate in the United States and Europe. But the government offers the settlers little service once they get here.

There is the Royal Mail, of course. In the Manola-Dunstable district it goes through with Jack Ellis travelling in a homemade cab with stovepipe peeping out the roof.

The government does not provide mail boxes. This homemade device near Viking serves all farms within five miles of Section 19, Township 49, Range 12, West of the Fourth Meridian.

But to a settler like Andrew Lupul, here outside his home thatched in the style of his native Ukraine (about 1902), the government offers a service that was never enjoyed by his ancestors in eastern Europe.

This document is an interim land title certificate. Once issued, it's good for three years and no one can push the holder off his land. If he builds a house and breaks so many acres, he gets a permanent title backed by the power of the national government. For Andrew Lupul, it's worth the exhausting journey from Russia to Canada.

This building represents the majesty of the Canadian federal presence, the Land Titles Office in Calgary, photographed on December 22nd, 1887, to show that the West is not necessarily in a permanent condition of snow and ice.

Competition for homestead land grows keen. That's the door of the land office at Grouard. A determined youth has bedded down, prepared to wait three days to be first in line.

Government at all levels maintains a low profile. A government service needs a tax base, and who wants to pay taxes? At the local level the first institution to which people are willing to pay tribute is the school. A school district has been formed to finance this log cabin standing in a clearing at Eidswold.

When there are enough kids around Red Deer Lake to require a teacher, tax money is needed to pay Miss Hawkey.

In 1889 residents of Medicine Hat form a public school district and build the first municipal hospital in the Territories. But a need to incorporate the municipality is not felt for another ten years.

A community without crime, without traffic, and without water or electrical systems can function without bureaucrats. Calgary wants to be different (incorporation 1884, school district 1886), but Edmonton votes for a school district in '84 and holds off incorporation until '92. The first municipal needs are usually limited to a town dump and a pound for stray animals. Around former trading posts like Edmonton there are packs of dogs, descendants of the sled dogs, shown in the frontispiece of Captain Butler's *The Wild North Land*, published 1872. Some Edmontonians build stiles rather than gates, to keep the dogs outside.

With the turn of the century, the population soars, to nearly one hundred and fifty thousand by 1905. The time has come to implement the dream of the Marquis of Lorne. On September 1st, 1905, the Province of Alberta will come into being. There'll be celebrations and celebrities. Coming for the inauguration ceremonies are Governor General Earl Grey and Prime Minister Sir Wilfrid Laurier, who has already proclaimed the twentieth century to belong to Canada. Over Jasper Avenue, out west at 103rd Street by the Hudson's Bay store, a triumphal arch goes up.

Another note of triumph is sounded by McDougall and Secord's department store at Jasper and 101st Street. A window display advertises the jolly fact that all these important people are coming to Edmonton for the ceremonies. Edmonton has won out over all rivals in the contest for seat of government. Arch-rival Calgary reaches for the prize but is informed by Mother Canada that she is too immature for such honour and responsibility.

The great moment draws near and so do the distinguished visitors. They're at Red Deer now, pausing for speeches on the station platform. The hosts strew something much better than roses at their feet. The platform sports a carpet of golden grain, fresh-grown on district farms.

Alberta's first day dawns blue and sunny. The parade moves up Jasper Avenue past the Alberta Hotel. The famous guests are staying there of course, in the capital's most modern and magnificent hostelry.

The small children are displayed prominently on wagons while older students walk in formation. Here a bevy of senior girls marches down McDougall Hill on the parade route to the fairgrounds... to hear Sir Wilfrid Laurier, the silver-tongued orator, proclaim the existence and shining prospects of Alberta.

September 1st, 1905 — a day to remember.

Rutherford, Railroads, and Reliability — The First Government

ON MARCH 15th, 1906, the Thistle Rink, largest assembly hall in the capital, is decked with bunting for the first speech of the first session of the first Alberta legislature. The majesty of British parliaments comes to a building where hockey fans throw coal on the ice to confuse the visiting team.

Lieutenant-Governor G.H.V. Bulyea reads the speech from the throne.

After the first session in a room of MacKay Avenue School, the twenty-five-man legislature and their families go on a tour of the province. Here they are at Raymond, visiting the Knight sugar-beet refinery.

Everywhere they meet enthusiasm, none more than at Vegreville, where the Bank of Commerce is happy to get by in a log hut until a proper bank is constructed. The bank inspector is not overly happy. Fearful of snakes, he sleeps on the counter when duty brings him to the town.

At all stops they leave a message contained in a variation of the three R's — Rutherford, Railroads, and Reliability. There's Premier Rutherford, known affectionately as Uncle Sandy, coming to work at the Old Terrace Building with a sheaf of plans for the new province.

The Rutherford government has almost no views on highways, except that autos shall yield to horses at intersections, and bridges shall be strong enough to support the weight of steam threshing machines like this monster with its attendant water wagon.

Railroads are the priority. When the province is formed it has 1,060 miles of railroad, making a map a very simple task for the artist illustrating a government report. By 1918 the map will be crowded with 4,519 miles of track. Alberta and Ottawa each has a dream about railroads.

Pursuing the national dream, Ottawa looks westward and backs two transcontinental lines through Edmonton and on to the coast via Jasper.

The railroads sprout townsites every eight to twelve miles. The Canadian Northern names many for company officials and their relatives. The Grand Trunk Pacific names towns in alphabetical order: Ryley, Shonts, Tofield.

The established village of Equity hauls its buildings nearly a mile to the railroad townsite called Ryley.

In 1910 an English writer named F. A. Talbot comes on this "hotel" in the bush and photographs it for his travel book *The New Garden of Canada.* "Scrupulously clean," he writes of the inn. His Chinese host informs Talbot that this is the first building in the railroad town of Edson. He's right.

While Ottawa sees a national purpose, Alberta pursues a provincial dream. Premier Rutherford (and his successors Arthur Sifton and Charles Stewart) argue that one mile of track opens twenty square miles of country — ten on each side. From 1905 to '18, 1,855 miles of track are laid with provincial guarantees of thirteen thousand to twenty-five thousand dollars per mile. While Ottawa looks east to west, dreamers of the provincial dream look fondly north — to the Peace River Country and the great waterways of the Athabasca-Mackenzie river system.

In the station at Lac La Biche passengers wait for a train and watch the departure of a Model-T on railway wheels. The converted Ford belongs to Mickey Ryan, who has a contract to haul mail on the route. Mickey will parlay this beginning into a fortune in northern mining.

Looking northwest, the Edmonton Dunvegan and British Columbia railway is chartered to bring steel to the Peace River Country, where the unsinkable *D.A. Thomas* serves communities along the mighty river. Once sunk and given up for lost, the doughty stern-wheeler is raised and returns to its home port with whistle blaring.

The lure of the big country is so great that settlers are forcing their way in over the trail from Edson.
At the end of the Edson Trail lies the town of Grande Prairie.

And beyond, at the foot of a hill with a magnificent view, the town of Peace River. The journey is in winter when the tortuous trail is paved with snow for sleigh runners. It is also made in late winter so that settlers will reach the promised land on the eve of spring.

This photo tells all about the booster spirit of the big country. It's titled *Cabbage and Boy Both Grown at Peace River Crossing* (the town later dropped the Crossing).

The ED & BC is nicknamed "The Ever Dangerous and Badly Constructed Railway," and the dream might have become a provincial nightmare. Alberta guaranteed twenty-two and a half million dollars in railway construction bonds. During the First World War, all railroads went bankrupt except the CPR, but the province didn't have to make good. By a marvellous stroke of luck, Ottawa took over all the bankrupt lines to form the Canadian National system and had to assume the debts as well.

So much for railroads, and all's well that ends well. As to reliability — when Mr. Rutherford vows to make the telephone available to every farm home even if it means running the mighty and entrenched Bell Telephone Company out of the province — you'd better believe him.

When Rutherford takes office, he finds but two long-distance lines in the province — Calgary to Edmonton and Lethbridge to Cardston — and seven farmers on one rural party line.

In 1908 the Bell system sells out under pressure, and telephone gangs like this — arranged on the pole in order of rank — fan out through the province to join the survey and railroad gangs. This crew is bringing rural phones to Crossfield, about 1910. They are young, footloose, and fancy free; many are just passing through. But the gangs provide employment for adventurous young fellows out from Ontario or Ohio or Scotland or Norway, sizing up Alberta as a place to settle.

And the system is sturdily built. When the Highwood River breaks off a pole at the base, the cableman rides serenely over the flood, supported by poles on either side.

In every community visited by the gang a small telephone office occupies a corner of a farmhouse or store. That's Nance Brimmacombe at the switchboard in a corner of Brimmacombe's Music Store, Vermilion.

The programme is interrupted by the war, but, when it is completed in 1922, Alberta has twenty thousand farmers with telephones and eight thousand miles of long-distance lines.

In pursuit of its promises, the regime is driven to more and more tracks and telephones by more and more people.

Midnight cannons saluting September 1st, 1905, are the starting guns for the rush. By the time the flow is stilled by Europe's "Guns of August" in 1914, the population triples to some four hundred and fifty thousand. Looking down from the Legislative Building — to this patch of river ice below the Fifth Street Bridge set for a traditional Ukrainian church service — men in government are reminded of the factors in this population. Of any six Albertans, three will have been born in Canada, one in the United States, one in the British Isles, and one in Europe.

Touring the New Cities

TWO OF THREE ALBERTANS are on farms, but the province develops five urban population centres that remain the big five for three-quarters of a century. In the first heady enthusiasm they develop identifying landmarks and institutions and civic personalities.

Let's have the boosters take us on a tour of their young cities. We'll start in the capital.

EDMONTON
Here's a tour bus now, loading behind the King Edward Hotel.

And here's our guide, telling us that little more than ten years ago Jasper Avenue looked like this — in 1903 when Charles M. Russell the American artist arrived.

He expected to paint scenes around a trading post and was disappointed to find such an up-to-date progressive town. At least that's what he told the editor of the *Bulletin*.

If only Russell could see Jasper Avenue now, in 1913 — here's the same view from a half block farther west. It's not always so crowded of course. There's a big parade today. The camera doesn't lie, but photographers have civic spirit. Rupert Brooke, the English poet, was here and wrote that "Edmonton is a quiet little town. . . ." Which shows that poets ought to stick to rhyming.

There's so much happening that three daily papers are needed to tell it all — the *Bulletin, Journal,* and *Capital.* You can get them at Mike's News Stand, on the sidewalk in front of the Bank of Nova Scotia. That's Mike in the middle, a hard-working lad from New York City and a real Edmonton booster. Keep an eye on Mike. He'll soon have an indoor stand.

Edmonton is as big as Chicago — in area that is, 144 square miles. The real-estate promoters have pushed it out in all directions. Those smart investors in the Cadillacs are being driven to see lots in the Summerland subdivision. Summerland is still outside the city, halfway to St. Albert.

Glenora is a high-priced neighbour-hood. A. B. Carruthers, the Montreal milling magnate, put Glenora on the market, and to give it the stamp of quality he donated the site for Government House, residence of Mr. Bulyea, the lieutenant-governor, and put a caveat on all the residential lots. If you build a house in Glenora you have to spend at least thirty-five hundred dollars.

The best stonemasons have come from Scotland to cut and shape the sandstone for the official buildings of the capital. They've been attracted by the wages of $2.25 a day. Here they are with one of the pillars for the Legislative Building.

It still looks pretty raw and un-finished, and the grounds have to be landscaped yet, but the dome is impressive through the arch of the High Level Bridge.

Here's the view from the dome with the bridge still under construction and the buildings of the University of Alberta across the river in the trees. In the foreground are the buildings of the old trading post,

which will be cleared away soon. As the Board of Trade says in its guide to the city, "Edmonton is too young a city to have any buildings of historical interest."

Here is the university up close. And isn't it a beauty! There are three halls of learning, Pembina, Assiniboia, and Athabasca.

Here is the south-side library, built by the City of Strathcona with a grant from Andrew Carnegie before amalgamation with Edmonton. We don't have a public library on the north side; turned it down. We claimed a population of fifty-three thousand. Carnegie offered a grant on his estimate of thirty-eight thousand, so we told him to keep it.

On the way back over town, the bus can stop for sightseeing and picture-taking right on the bridge, as these young women have done. There's little difference anyway between being at a stop and the speed limit of three miles an hour.

There's more to see. We've got a Flatiron Building just like New York, only it's not as tall. And in the background is the steel for the McLeod Building.

Here's the Tegler Building. In the sketch it looks even more impressive than it really is. Tegler never gets around to putting the third section on the left rear.

This is the Brown Block, part of the Pantages Theatre, which later becomes the Strand. Brown never gets around to putting up the other eight stories of the office tower, but he has the booster spirit. You're either a booster or a knocker.

These signs tell it all. So enjoy your visit. Come again, and bring your investment capital.

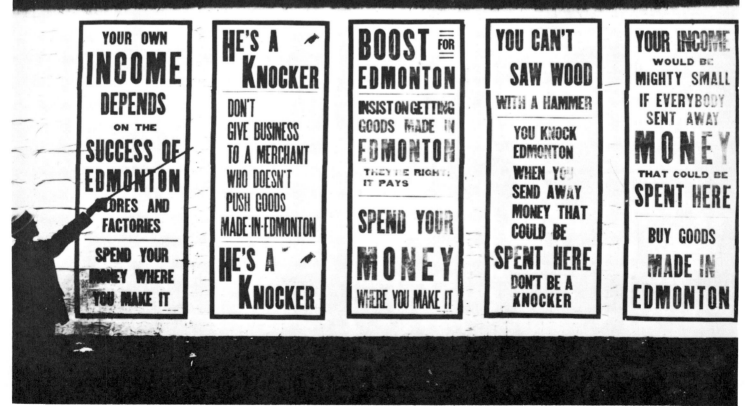

RED DEER

This is the city of Red Deer, looking west along Ross Street to the new railroad station.

A passenger steps down from the train for a platform stretch and spies a sign above the Gaetz Department Store: Trains Stop 12 Minutes. Plenty Time for Refreshments at Olympia Café.

In the Olympia the stranger is spotted at once by a local booster who regales him with the joys of investment in the Red Deer valley.

There are many good opportunities here in which a smart fellow could invest. That's Frank Van Slyke behind his patented mouldboard plough. You'll find a number of those in the district. The Van Slyke plough is made by the Standard Iron Works in Edmonton because we don't have a foundry — yet.

Sir Wilfrid Laurier is one of our boosters. You should have been here on August 19th, 1910, when he came as prime minister and drove the first spike on Red Deer's own railway — the Alberta Central, promoted by Red Deer financiers.

You'll hardly find a museum in the whole province because people are more interested in the future and anything old goes to the dump, but we have a Natural History Museum in Red Deer. That's some use. Dr. George's museum is full of stuffed owls and badgers and things from the Red Deer valley. (The very animals Kerry Wood will write about a half-century further on.)

We have higher education here. This is Red Deer Ladies College, with the girls decked out in their Sunday finest. But if you could see the staff, you'd see that the girls stick to business. And business is good in Red Deer. Well, the conductor is calling "All aboard!" Your twelve minutes are up. But come back and bring your capital!

SOME OF THE STUDENTS.

CALGARY

Calgary has an open-air streetcar for sightseeing. One hour of Calgary for twenty-five cents. Of course the foothills city offers many golden opportunities for investment.

Dan Finlayson is the constable on traffic duty at Calgary's busiest intersection — Eighth Avenue and First Street West. The lady is asking Dan where to catch the sightseeing car and he says, "Right here, ma'am. Comes by once an hour. Almost all the cars pass here."

That's the official street railway clock on the corner pole. This is called the Alexander Corner, because of the big sandstone building, a good example of why Calgary is called the Sandstone City. When Edmonton stole the capital, they had to come here to get the sandstone for Government House and the Legislative Building. Did you know that Calgary had a sandstone exhibit in the Chicago World's Fair of 1893? The city put in a carving of a giant bassinet. Won a prize of course.

The city hall is sandstone. It looks even more impressive lighted up to greet the Duke of Connaught.

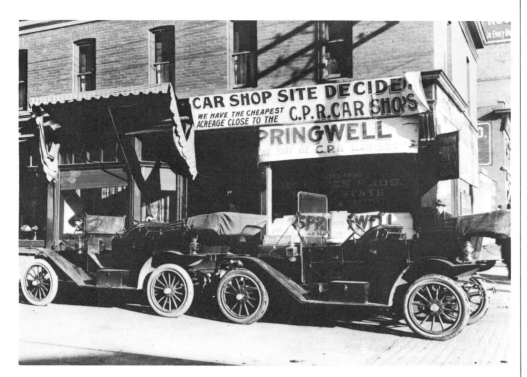

They think they've got real estate to sell in Edmonton, but we have the best opportunities, as you can see advertised at any office. This banner means that the CPR has decided on Ogden as the site for its repair shops, and smart investors will want land in the Springwell subdivision which is close by — well, not too far off anyway.

I'm sure you'll agree that we've got more of a *city* than Edmonton. We've got a skyline, as you'll see when the streetcar brings you down Centre Street for a look at the new bridge. The bridge is going to have stone lions on the railings. There'll be some class to that.

Here's a post card showing *A Calgary Skyscraper — The Grain Exchange Building* . . . .

Of course you can see the Palliser Hotel. Here's the Palliser with the new Canadian Pacific Railway depot alongside. The photographer must have taken this on a Sunday, because the scene ought to be swirling with people.

Then there's the Hudson's Bay Company — has a real metropolitan look.

Ten years ago the Bay had a kind of country store, and this was the grocery department. Orange Meat? (That was Corn Flakes.) And Tetley's Tea came in three-pound cans and sold for a dollar. The photographer took twenty minutes to get this time exposure. Only one customer came in. The clerks kept moving while they filled his order, so they don't show in the picture.

Well you can see how much has happened here in ten years. Here comes your open-air streetcar, ma'am. Come again and bring your capital.

LETHBRIDGE

Something must be out of time
sequence here; are we not looking at
Klondike Days in Edmonton? Not
on your life. These girls are perform-
ing at the race track at the Lethbridge
Fair in 1912. Even in 1912 Lethbridge
is Alberta's third largest city —
seventeen thousand people — and
Lethbridge has it all.

Look at this news vendor. His stock
ranges from prayer books to the
Calgary *Eye Opener* and the *Ladies
Home Journal* to Wild West pulp
magazines. You can't have more of
everything than that!

Edmonton thinks it has a High Level Bridge — 157 feet high. But try the view, if you have a steady stomach, from our CPR viaduct. You're gazing down 307 feet to the Oldman River.

And the viaduct runs one mile and forty-seven feet — five times as long and twice as high as Edmonton's midget bridge.

Lethbridge is the only place outside Calgary and Edmonton with street-cars. This one appears to have a Mounted Police escort, which it deserves. Electric trolley cars are the sure sign that a town has arrived as a city.

Lethbridge has civic style. Land is worth money, so come back with your capital because it's going to be worth more. Even so, we have a park in the heart of the city, Galt Park, named for Sir Alexander Tilloch Galt, the coal baron.

Yes, Lethbridge is known as the City That Coal Built, and in the yards of the CPR station those are cars of the Northwest Coal and Navigation Company. And thereby hangs a tale....

COAL

Later on, when trees have grown up in Galt Park (July 18th, 1928), the city organizes a tribute to the pioneers of its basic industry. On the platform are the widow and daughter of Alberta's first coal-mine operator, Nicholas Sheran.

In 1870 this young Irishman was driving a whisky trader's wagon between Fort Benton, Montana, and Fort Whoop-Up. He recognized a coal seam in the high, soft banks and made his return trips with a load of coal. In 1872 he opened the first mine.

The entrance to Sheran's drift would have looked like this one, photographed in 1881 by the Dominion Geological Survey visiting the community known as Coalbanks.

Edmonton finds that a coal mine is a poor foundation on which to build a school — if the mine is too close to the surface and coal has been taken out. Here is the first brick school in Edmonton, built in 1895 and demolished for safety when the old coal workings cave in beneath it. (The site is marked by a plaque between the AGT Tower and McDougall Church.)

In 1899 the CPR builds an important line from Fort Macleod to Nelson, B.C., opening up the mineral resources of the Crowsnest Pass. To finance the line, the CPR accepts a grant of eleven thousand dollars per mile from the federal government and in return agrees to haul prairie grain at a cheaper rate to ports on Lake Superior and the Pacific Ocean. The coking ovens at Coleman become a favourite subject for nocturnal photography.

Three major disasters strike the Crowsnest mines. One hundred and eighty-nine lives are lost in a cave-in at Hillcrest on June 19th, 1914. In December, thirty-one die at Bellevue. Another disaster takes place in the open. This is the town of Frank in 1902, looking along Dominion Avenue toward Turtle Mountain.

In April 1903 the face of the mountain falls. One hundred million tons of rock crash on the east end of the town, leaving sixty-six dead. A few days after the fall, the bare face of the mountain frames a parade of miners who were trapped and who are now out of harm.

One of the storied coal promoters is Sam Drumheller, who gives his name to one of Alberta's coal centres. Sam is a great showman. Early roads into the deep valley are not the most reliable. Sam is at the wheel of a new Cadillac that he has driven to town — along the ice of the Red Deer River, all the way from Red Deer.

Mining communities of the old world are found traditionally in narrow, pinched valleys. In Alberta they are often set in mountain grandeur, like Nordegg, town of the Brazeau River collieries.

Coal production in Alberta rises from three hundred thousand tons in 1900 to nearly seven million tons in 1920. The railroads build an extension known as the Coal Branch into the valley of the McLeod River. Miners at Cadomin live in picturesque log cabins cut from the virgin lodgepole pine. British capital is at work here. The name Cadomin comes from the cable address of Canadian Dominion Mine.

Luscar is an intensely competitive community. Eventually the demand for coal will drop and Luscar will be razed to the ground and levelled like ancient Carthage. Of all the industries to rise from the ashes, coal seems the least probable. But it will.

MEDICINE HAT

Welcome to Medicine Hat. More people have heard about us than have heard about Calgary and Edmonton. For one thing, we've got the best publicity man. Rudyard Kipling, the English poet, is one of our boosters. For an English poet, he's a lot sharper than Rupert Brooke. Kipling called us "the town that was born lucky."

Maybe you want advice about investing your capital. Well, just go along to the Assiniboia Hotel. It's our finest of course. You'll find the lobby illuminated by natural gas from our local wells. And when you get there, ask for Captain Horatio Ross. Captain Ross inherited capital from wealthy parents who lived in a castle in Scotland. In '98 he sailed down river from Calgary on a steam launch he'd built himself. He planned to stop overnight only, but it was his birthday and he was made so welcome that he stayed and built the Assiniboia Hotel and many other things.

We're in the centre of a very dynamic ranching and farming district. Too bad Rudyard Kipling couldn't have been here to see the big tractor parade on the main streets.

In the United States they have a saying, "We get our weather from Medicine Hat." That's because the telegraph agent in the station here gathers the weather reports from all the stations on the CPR and it all goes into the papers under our date line. Those are Americans in the parade of cars. They're up from Colorado to look at farmland near Gem.

Rudyard Kipling was taken out to Redcliff when he came here in '03. He called it "the brickfield." That's a poet for you. He wrote about "the ribs and frames of the brick-making mechanism... the rest was prairie, the mere curve of the earth with little grey birds calling."

They flared the gas wells in his honour. Sights like this inspired him to write that "Medicine Hat has all hell for a basement." And thereby hangs a tale....

OIL AND GAS

The gas in Medicine Hat's basement is discovered in 1883 when a railroad worker strikes a match over a well thought to contain water only. He is merely surprised by the discovery. Natural gas jets in many areas give promise of a gas and oil industry. On September 21st, 1902, petroleum flows at three hundred barrels a day from this hillside near Waterton Park. Drillers have gone down 1,020 feet to find it. A cluster of shacks supporting Alberta's first commercial well is called Oil City.

It's early. The Imperial Oil Company is still in the horse and buggy days.

Wildcatting requires a climate of optimism. Alberta certainly provides the climate for pioneer drillers like "Tiny" Phillips.

With minimum encouragement, the drillers fight on, come hell or high water from spring floods at this Southern Alberta Land Company well.

Communities are intrigued by natural gas and the potential for clean, low-cost heat. Castor inaugurates a town gas system supplied by its own municipal well.

This ceremony is the actual start of the Viking gas field, summer of 1914. The shovel operator is W.J. Magrath, president of the Edmonton Industrial Association, whose members have subscribed one hundred dollars apiece to develop a municipal gas supply. Surveys indicate a major gas field containing enough to heat Edmonton for a century. The boosters are mistaken about the amount of money required for development, but they're right about the gas. It's down there.

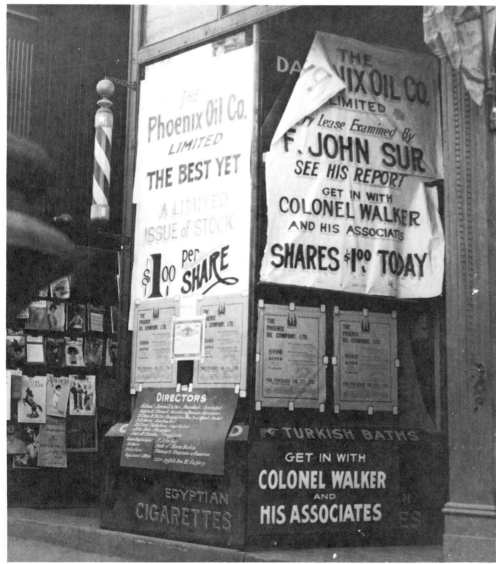

Gas excites communities, but individual investors are inspired by oil. In May 1914 oil fever grips Calgary. Investors wait their turn with impatience.

For only a dollar you can get in with Colonel Walker, Calgary's Man of the Century.

The oil boom provides employment for artists. They decorate shares with volcanic gushers that later in the century would result in a call to Red Adair.

And what's causing the excitement? A. W. Dingman's discoveries at Turner Valley. Dingman Number One is by the river, with Number Two and room for more beyond.

On July 28th, 1914, Mr. Dingman (right) welcomes distinguished company to his discovery, Governor General the Duke of Connaught, the Duchess of Connaught, and Princess Patricia who accepts a bottle of black gold from T. A. P. Frost. The duke's expression indicates that this is all frightfully interesting, but he'll not be buying shares. The discoveries by Dingman and his fellow adventurers are modest and scattered, but they keep alive the promise of something big.

BASSANO, BEST LITTLE TOWN BY A DAM SITE

Welcome to Bassano, friend. It's not a city because you need fifteen hundred people for a city charter. But we have the best little town by a dam site. . . . And thereby hangs a tale of irrigation.

Senator Coté could tell you about irrigation — just as he told the Easterner. The Easterner was claiming that Alberta was no good for agriculture. And Senator Coté set him straight, "No, no, my friend, it is good land. But in the north you must take water off the land and put it in the river, and in the south you must take water off the river and put it on the land."

Here is the dam site in 1911. You can see what the CPR is doing, building a reservoir on the Bow River to irrigate its land grants in this area. The land is good but dry.

The senator could tell the story about the first big scheme, back in the nineties, to put the St. Mary's River out on the land. You can see how the land needs it. Most of the water is behind those gates.

Pity the poor cowboy who comes upon this monster after a night that's anything but dry. A steam-powered dredge claws its way across land on which the senator says water must be put.

What ho for a voyage of inspection on a CPR irrigation ditch? Distin-guished company has come aboard — Sir Edmund Walker, general manager of the Bank of Commerce. Any available flags are flown be-cause these are heady days. These are the days of real sport.

The Days of Real Sport

"THERE IS MUCH TEA and tennis, golf, 'mobiling, dancing, dining and wild riding across the hills; for when people are healthy and prosperous they are instinctively hospitable, and always in a big-handed, big-hearted way." This is Emily Ferguson Murphy in the book *Janey Canuck in the West*, recording her impressions on moving to Alberta in 1908.

Alberta is a young province with a young population. Homesteading, politics, and the real estate business are attacked with the zest of youth, as are tea, tennis, golf, 'mobiling, dancing, dining, and wild riding across the hills.

Tea can be a grand business indeed. The Duchess of Connaught, wife of the governor general, is the guest of honour at a 1912 lawn party in the gardens of Premier Arthur Sifton. Mrs. Sifton is on the front line, fifth from the left. The duchess is next, under a hat with feathers enough to join a flight of migrating birds. The tall girl at her side is Canada's sweetheart, age twenty-six, Her Royal Highness the Princess Patricia.

Tennis of fiercely competitive nature is about to break forth at Bow Valley Ranch. This is "lawn" tennis on buffalo grass. Ranch owner W. Roper Hull, in black beard, chats with the contestants.

The community of Coalspur might seem better suited to wild riding across the hills. But Coalspur has a tennis club.

Calgary city champion A. Carson McWilliams blasts a drive from the eleventh tee of the municipal golf course.

Edmonton golfers reminisce about their first clubhouse, the old Big House of Fort Edmonton. During the last outbreak of smallpox (1901), the clubhouse was converted to an isolation hospital and was burned down afterwards. Stamped out the disease — smallpox that is.

'Mobiling can make the heart pound with excitement. Speeds of thirty miles an hour are possible on the rolling hills of the short-grass country near High River. But a patch of swampy ground can immobilize flying wheels and subject the adventurous to the humiliation of rescue by a team of oxen.

It's a fine day in 1907, and there'll be dancing all the way to Galt Island even if the decks of S.S. *City of Medicine Hat* are so crowded that the orchestra has to play from a barge being towed behind. And there's a dance pavilion waiting on the island four miles upstream.

Dining is high fashion on the terrace of the Macdonald Hotel, out-of-doors on a long summer evening. Albertans are newcomers still revelling in the novelty of extended summer days.

And speak of wild riding across the hills — what could be wilder than this? A prairie coyote, standing in for the proper English fox, has been sighted heading across Weasel Head Bridge, and here come the pursuers in full cry and in full attire for a hunt on English fields.

Banff has it all, plus magnificent peaks and one mountain that gushes hot sulphur water. Banff is Canada's first national park, designated in 1887. A horse-drawn bus leaves the original Banff Springs Hotel, bound perhaps for the hot springs which are good for what ails the well-to-do.

Of course there's more to life than tea and tennis, golf, 'mobiling, dancing, dining, and wild riding across the hills. At Canmore, near the entrance to Banff National Park, the girls have their own hockey team.

When winter comes to Lethbridge, the vigorous can take the streetcar to Henderson's Lake for an afternoon of skating.

There's skating year-round at Sherman's Roller Rink in Calgary, as well as big events like the concert by Dame Nellie Melba — until the fire.

Curlers compete for big prizes, really big ones. Messrs. Orsum, Fairley, Wilson, and Lundy have established supremacy at the Innisfail Bonspiel.

On summer days in Edmonton it costs the kids nothing to wait with bare feet in the gutter for the street-railway flushing car to send cool delicious waves washing over their toes.

Vaudeville is at its peak with travelling acts like the Juvenile Bostonians, but they play only the major cities.

Moving pictures on film can be shown in the smaller centres. In 1910 a crowd in the Innisfail Opera House waits for the movie to begin.

For miles around Alix, the Alix Citizen's Band will contribute to any occasion.

Civic pride is the prize when baseball teams compete. The scene is Wiste, south of Consort on the Sedalia line, where the ballplayers of Wiste are meeting the challenge of another town.

At the Esdale Press picnic in Edmonton the ladies compete at tug o' war.

Ladies are not admitted to the long rooms, where gleaming mirrors reflect the shine of mahogany bar tops and brass cuspidors. The Alberta Hotel in Crossfield has such a room.

Bars are financial exchanges where wagers may be placed on the outcome of manly athletic events like this one, in 1913, at Hillhurst Park. The Calgary Tigers (forerunners of the Stampeders) are playing a match of rugby football, perhaps against the Edmonton Eskimos. These teams will meet later for the provincial championship, but they will meet in Red Deer because neither will play on the home ground of the other.

The grandstand at the Calgary Exhibition grounds is witness to the sport of kings in the summer. In winter it's adapted for an exhilarating pastime imported from Norway.

Calgary Stampede

IN 1912 THE GROUNDS are the scene of rousing sport that arouses resentment in a large sector of the business community. It may seem strange that the builders of the city would take umbrage at an event which spreads the magic name of Calgary.

The posters explain.

In 1908 Calgary stages the Dominion Exhibition, and the theme of the poster is a cowboy finding "another trail cut off" — another trail closed by a farm or factory fence. The sign on the post reads: Visit Alberta before the Golden Opportunities, Picturesque Riders, and Indians are Gone.

Then, four years later, this blossoms everywhere — the cowboys and Indians aren't dead. In fact, the Wild Bunch will be whooping and hollering for a whole week, less than a mile from City Hall. "We are not amused," say many civic leaders. "This is terrible for Calgary's image."

vel

at record ski season — if there's snow

e near Banff: Olympic factor

ympics cials say the new lift system will y, in-mean year-round skiing at the top.

druple   Also expanding snow-making is st of Lake Louise. Other areas, such as Whistler, Big White near Kelowna

and Cypress Bowl in West Vancouver, are improving access to their high alpine areas.

Mike Duggan, a marketing expert for the Canada West Ski Operators' Association, says that early advance sales of season passes and tour bookings are up again this year.

He says other operators will be watching the popularity of Blackcomb's lift system.

"The biggest problem for them is 'can we afford it?' The technology is dropping in price but they will need the (skier) volume."

They will also be watching the effect of the Winter Olympics on the Banff-Lake Louise area, which set records for skier visits last year.

"There will be a lessening of vol-

ume during the two-week period of the Olympics because there is a lack of beds for skiers," Duggan said. "The publicity of the Olympics could be offset by people saying the areas will be real busy and they won't go there this year."

Lift ticket prices are rising in some areas — a day ticket at Whistler-Blackcomb now is $31 compared with $28 last year — and Duggan says operators are trying to recoup investments in equipment.

Duggan points out that Aspen, Colo., charges the equivalent of $39 Cdn for a day pass, Squaw Valley, Calif., $37 and Sun Valley, Idaho, $36.

Season passes, package tours, frequent-user passes and other

promotions can cut costs by one-third, said Duggan. At Silver Star, near Vernon, B.C., 16 of every 25 skiers last year were using discounts and the average lift ticket was 67 per cent of full price.

"There's value out there, you just have to look for it," said Duggan.

Those seeking Okanagan powder can expect to pay about $25 for a day ticket. A sample package that includes air fare from Vancouver, lifts and lodging for five days starts at $289 per person based on quadruple occupancy at Big White.

Whistler is $435 with a Calgary departure but that can go to $580 in the Christmas period and from Feb. 1 to April 26.

Promoter Guy Weadick needs the support and participation of many friends to make the Stampede go. One is Mrs. Weadick, known professionally as Flores La Due, World Champion Fancy Roper. Flores is demonstrating how to rope a "critter" while lying on the ground.

Another supporter is A. E. Cross, president of Calgary Brewing. That's Guy Weadick in the black Stetson. The chap in the cap is Hoot Gibson, star of western movies, who is making a film on Guy's ranch.

Despite Guy's friends, acceptance is slow. Not until 1923 will the Stampede gain respectability and merge with the Exhibition.

Note the man on the left. He's a famous artist visiting some Indian chiefs at the Stampede. He, too, is a friend of Guy. On his return home he writes the following thank-you note:

Great Falls, Montana
Friend Guy:

I received your postal and letter an was glad to here from you: You were so bussy when I left I did not get to thank you for the good time we had at the Stampede. I came west 31 years ago, at that time baring the Indians an a fiew scatered whites the country belonged to God but now the real estate man an nester have got moste of it grass side down an most of the cows that are left feed on shuger beet pulp but thank God I was here first an in my time Iv seen som roping and riding but never before have I seen so much of it bunched as I did at Calgary. Ive seen som good wild west showes but I couldent call what you pulled off a show. It was the real thing an a whole lot of it . . . .

With best wishes from your friend
C. M. Russell.

World War

IN THE LATE SUMMER OF 1914 the mood of exuberance turns to one of anger, anger given blunt expression on a Calgary grocer's truck. Odd about the object of the sign painter's hate. Odd that the Kaiser should be a nephew of Princess Louise Caroline Alberta, for whom the province is named.

An army band plays fighting music on a street corner of Medicine Hat.

The farewells begin. In the second month of the war recruits not yet in uniform leave Lethbridge.

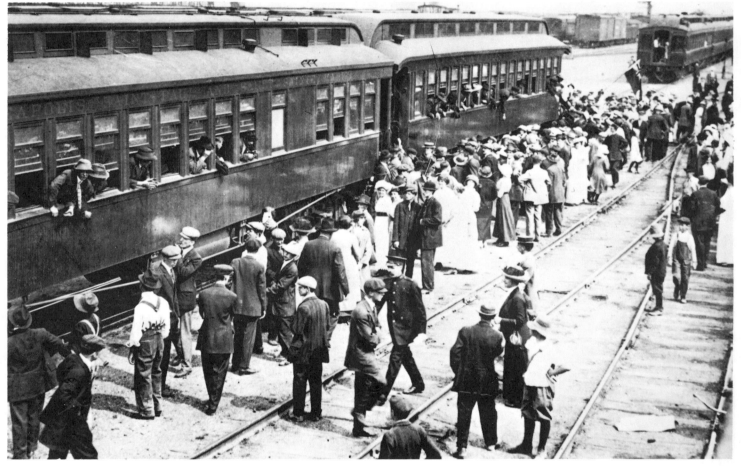

ST CONTINGENT
LEAVING
YOUNGSTOWN
ALTA.

ONE OF THE BUFFALO BOYS
SPINNING A ROPE

BELL Photo

All trains, it seems, come to take away the young and vigorous. On the wind-swept station yard at Youngstown the first contingent awaits the train. Behind them the flag snaps to attention over a raw main street that many will never see again.

The recruits are willing and able. A few are battle-ready, including Henry Nor'west. Henry is a Métis rodeo performer who does roping and trick-shooting. Camp life and the role of sharpshooter are old stuff to Henry, who becomes a renowned sniper.

On the Blood Reserve at Fort Macleod there are volunteers for the
191st Battalion. George Coming
Singer is the young man at the top
left. George will not return.

Alberta sends four cavalry units in
the opening months of the conflict.
These officers are buying mounts for
the 19th Alberta Dragoons.

This may explain the cavalry's readiness: the 15th Alberta Light Horse drawn up in parade order on the plain of Sarcee. The 15th is a militia troop organized by a Calgary alderman to maintain a tradition set by western horsemen in the war in South Africa. Four squadrons make it up — from Calgary, Cochrane, High River, and Innisfail.

The exhilarating cavalry ride is the very spirit of the ranch country. Near Innisfail, a group of ranch people gather for a coyote hunt. Even the ladies are prepared for wild riding across the hills, properly sidesaddle of course.

In the early months, the war itself seems real sport. The army takes over the buildings of the new Edmonton Exhibition grounds. Recruits practice digging trenches on the infield of the race track. On Sunday visitors come out for tea.

On May 10th, 1915, spectators watch from the hillside above Victoria Park as the 49th Battalion, the 51st Battalion, and the Canadian Mounted Rifles receive their colours.

Amid cheers and songs, the battalions march to their trains and are carried away — to inconceivable disaster, a stalemate of vast armies which destroy but cannot move each other. On this newsboard at Jasper and 101st Street the terrible story is recorded — year after year and battle after inconclusive battle. The frightful cost is measured by casualty lists. Long sheets hang on the board, with names and numbers of young men dead, wounded, and missing. They hang there until the next attack creates a new list.

There's a long, long trail of disillusion, so hard and so bewildering that those who travel it will never be able to retrace it and find again the world of sunlit certainties that existed in 1914. For the province of Alberta, that world was the time of youth.

The War is Over

AFTER FOUR YEARS and three months, the terrible conflict ends. So much prestige and honour have been trampled into the torn battleground. The high-spirited glamour of the cavalry has come to humiliation against mud and barbed wire, but a new elite has arisen from grass fields behind the lines.

Fred McCall and his aviation stunts
are the big attraction of the 1919
exhibition.

In the summer of 1919 the skies over Alberta fairgrounds buzz with war-surplus training planes flown by the new air heroes. Calgary's ace is Captain Fred McCall, victor in thirty-seven air battles.

Fred is forced to improvise a stunt when his Curtiss "Jenny" loses power on a swoop past the grandstand. He puts it down with little damage to the merry-go-round, the plane, or McCall — for whom the city will eventually name its international airport.

Jock Palmer is the hero of the City That Coal Built. In 1922 Jock sets out in this "Jenny" to pioneer an international mail route from Lethbridge to Ottawa. Though Jock is unhurt when the plane tangles with telephone wires at Minot, North Dakota, the crash writes *finis* to the plane, the undertaking, and Lethbridge Flying Services, a spiritual ancestor of Time Air.

The Avro 504 (below) is an ancestor of the Chieftain Air Bus. War hero Keith Tailyeur persuades Scottish cab operator Jock McNeill that the time has come for an Edmonton-Calgary air taxi. The venture has too many problems, not least of which is lubricating the delicate rotary engine. It subjects the lone passenger to a fine spray of castor oil.

The *City of Edmonton* ''Jenny'' hangs over the spring horse show in 1919, from the ceiling of a building built for horse shows and converted by necessity into an arena (later known as the Edmonton Gardens), the city's major sports palace until the Coliseum opens in 1974.

The plane is leased to Wop May, a local boy who was involved in the last air battle of Germany's legendary Red Baron.

Stunting airplanes are not the only motorized attraction at the fairgrounds. Autos displace horses on the race track. Imperial Oil wants to advertise that it's out of the horse and buggy era.

A keen spectator at the aerial exhibitions is the man in the black hat, Charlie Taylor, Imperial's head northern geologist.

Charlie is regulating the flow from this important discovery well, at Fort Norman, on the Mackenzie River. He believes it is possible to harness the new air power for transporting men and equipment between Alberta and the far north.

Imperial buys two Junkers freight planes from Germany. That's Charlie in the fur coat. The pilots are war veterans Elmer Fullerton (second from the left) and George Gorman (second from the right). Aircraft, alas, are not yet dependable enough for heavy long-distance work. The Fort Norman experiment is a failure and such a bitter disappointment for Charlie Taylor that he takes his own life.

Aviation reverts to the military for further development. The Royal Canadian Air Force opens a prairie base at High River, and Fullerton re-enters the service as a pilot.

Stunts are still what aircraft can do best. Here's Fullerton participating in a stunt involving radio. From the cockpit of his Avro Viper, he's being heard on the first air-to-ground broadcast over CFCN. He is reciting the dramatic closing chapter in the life of Dangerous Dan McGrew.

Farm Power

ON THE EVENING OF JULY 18TH, 1921, spectators jam the street in front of the *Edmonton Journal.* This is the last provincial election before radio, and they have come to watch the results on a second-storey scoreboard. They will witness the emergence of the province's second political dynasty as the United Farmers of Alberta virtually obliterate the founding Liberal regime and begin fourteen years in power.

Seventy-two percent of Albertans live in rural areas. Tonight marks the achievement of one goal in a campaign that began here in Mechanics Hall, Edmonton, in January 1909. Standing on the platform are the senior officers of two bodies which are merging to become the UFA — the Alberta Farmers Association and the Farmers Society of Equity.

United by formal resolution, they make a symbolic march over downtown streets to the legislature. It's the beginning of a march for power: political, social, and economic.

In the summer, the unity of farm people is promoted by annual picnics. This is the 1916 picnic of the Pine Lake local. An ingenious member has heightened the festival air with a merry-go-round made of poplar trunks.

The long winters are livened by policy meetings. The meeting advertised here brings to a single platform two of the dynamic leaders of the farm movement.

When Henry Wise Wood came from Missouri in 1905, he brought with him years of experience in the populist politics of American farm states. With an inspiring message about the power of co-operation, Wood has given structure to the movement in Alberta. His farm is at Carstairs.

J. E. Brownlee is to become the premier of Alberta from 1925 to '33.

Big Valley to Munson District
U. F. A. Association ANNUAL
CONVENTION

WILL BE HELD IN

BIG VALLEY

...on...

Nov 10th at Noon

Speakers:- **PRESIDENT WOOD**
J. E. BROWNLEE, U. F. A. Legal Adviser

Every Local is requested to make it a point to send their full quota of delegates to this important meeting. Delegates should hand their names to the Secretary before the meeting opens. Locals have the privilege of submitting resolutions to this convention.

Election of Officers for the coming year

Pres. P. J. Rock, Morrin - Sec'y-Treas. E. J. Garland, Rumsey

MAIL QUICK PRINT, DRUMHELLER

Mr. Brownlee, Calgary lawyer, is also legal adviser to the United Grain Growers, a farmer-owned company leading the fight to break the monopoly of the Winnipeg Grain Exchange in marketing prairie grain crops.

Fight is the word for it. The private operators think grain growers should stick to their traditional role. After the harvest, portrayed with such charm by J. H. Gano of Wainwright, they should devote their energies to merry peasant dances and leave the marketing (and the merry profits) to the grain barons.

The barons are able to exert fierce pressure, but railroad sidings all across the prairies see the rise of UGG elevators that mean economic power for the farmers.

A new Alberta-only marketing co-op raises a booth on the midway of the Calgary Stampede and the model elevator crowning the booth has real-life counterparts.

With each Pool elevator built, there is satisfaction, but when a private elevator is taken over, and the name is painted out and replaced by the Pool sign, satisfaction runneth over. This commercial elevator at Shonts is destined to give that pleasure. (Later, it is destined to be moved into Heritage Park, Calgary, to represent all grain elevators.)

Through the 1920s, the sun shines on Alberta. What is more important, the rain falls. And most important, prices are good — a dollar a bushel for wheat.

The most popular young man in the world joins the fraternity of Alberta farm folk. Here he is on a visit to his ranch near High River, with George Webster, mayor of Calgary. It's the Prince of Wales, destined to be King Edward VIII.

In autumn the railroads run harvester excursions from eastern Canada to provide helping hands for the harvest, and quality is good too. Herman Trelle, a Pool member, becomes World Wheat King for crops grown on his farm at Wembley in the Peace River Country.

Slim Moorhouse of Buffalo Hills makes an annual event of delivering the crop to elevators at Vulcan. Slim's specialty is harnessing big teams. On November 27th, 1922, he has thirty horses pulling eight wagons loaded with 1,144 bushels of wheat. This is horsemanship of a high order, so skilful that in 1925 Slim is invited to perform at the Calgary Stampede. From Gleichen all the way to the Stampede grounds, he drives ten wagons hitched to thirty-six matched Percherons.

Women Are People

IN GOVERNMENT THE UNITED FARMERS are populists. They're against special class legislation (unless it's in their own self-interest, such as guaranteeing prices offered by the wheat pools) and so reject a bill allowing Imperial Oil to build a pipeline from Fort McMurray. They're against privilege and regard the University of Alberta, and its new medical school, as bastions of privilege. Despite open threats of closure, the medical faculty makes its mark.

Although the UFA lacks the creative vision of the first dynasty, there are no railroads or telephone lines left to build. And they do have a good grasp on human rights. When they take power in 1921, they find themselves involved in a socio-legal question with implications that run far beyond the borders of Alberta.

The question has been raised, half in jest, by this man, a lawyer named Harry Robertson. The question concerns the status of women. Are women people? In Canadian law are women to be considered *persons* with the privileges of men? The Supreme Court of Canada says not. "Women are equal with regard to pains and penalties but not with regard to privileges," it intones, implying: What could be more sensible than that?

The view may be sound Canadian law but is unacceptable in the Province of Alberta. Alberta has a brief history, but women have earned equality by their contribution to its making.

The homemaker role has demanded more in a pioneer setting. Washday at a sod farmhouse is demonstrated by Florence Lewis and Mrs. John Larson of Delia.

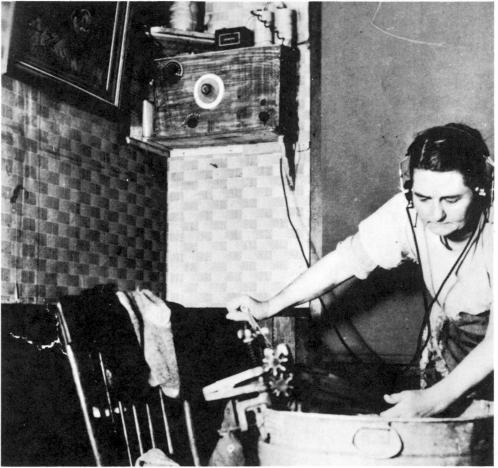

In fact, even in a modern frame house with a radio for company, washday is heavy duty.

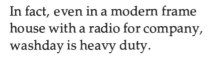

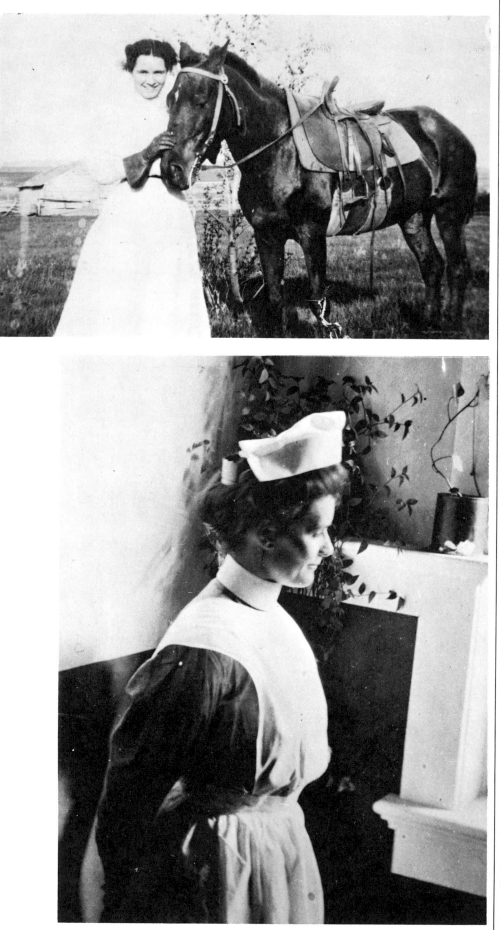

The traditional career roles of teacher and nurse have also demanded more. Isabelle Dawson is the teacher at Frozen Nose Corner in the Springbank district. Isabelle is so popular with the kids and parents that they've made her a gift of a saddle horse (about 1905).

When the UFA takes office, this serene nurse is Alberta's first lady, Louise Hungerford Brett, wife of the second lieutenant-governor (1915-25). The picture is from early days in Banff, where she and Dr. Brett founded the Banff Sanitarium in 1886.

More young women have been coming into new career roles in business. Students of the Edmonton Commercial School pose with the tools of their profession and their principal, J. Percy Page, who will become Alberta's eighth lieutenant-governor in 1960.

Women have asserted their right to equality under the Homestead Act. Sabrine Jacobsen and Josephine Solberg have title to their own farms in the district known as Square Deal.

The main line of the Grand Trunk Pacific is acknowledged to be the best-built railroad grade in western Canada. Women contractors handled part of the grade near Viking, hats and all.

Women's Institutes, like this group at Fort Macleod, have been upgrading the quality of life in rural areas. WIs are chartered under provincial legislation and receive operating grants.

On June 17th, 1917, Alberta women invaded another male preserve. These ladies are at the polling booth at Westcott, near Didsbury, to participate in the provincial election. By this time everyone thought women should vote.

That is, everyone but Boudreau. Lucien Boudreau, MLA for St. Albert, nicknamed "Little Napoleon," was the only one to vote against women's suffrage when it was proposed in the legislature.

The contribution of women to the effort of a nation at war cleared the last serious opposition. This pleasant country road is 40th Avenue South, in Calgary. Those are three society women driving a wagon to collect bottles and cans for the Prisoner-of-War Fund.

Alberta nurses served in the war zone. In 1917 Sister Roberta McAdams was elected to the legislature as a soldier representative. Home from the war, she is seen with other MLAs still in uniform.

Women have the vote, but they still have a problem — of legal status. This is a job for *The Famous Five*.

THE FAMOUS FIVE

Alberta has the first women magistrates in the British Empire, appointed in 1916. There is Alice Jamieson in Calgary and in Edmonton Emily Murphy, "Janey Canuck." This is Mrs. Murphy's court, where Harry Robertson raised the question that became a matter of social conscience for the UFA government. Harry argued that she was not qualified to be a magistrate because she was not a *person* under the British North America Act. He was only half serious but turned out to be right. Emily had to fight back, and she gathered some friends.

An obvious ally was Nellie McClung (in black), here chatting with the most famous suffragette in the world, Britain's Emily Pankhurst, on a visit to Edmonton in 1916 — the very day of Mrs. Murphy's appointment. Nellie McClung is armed with the good humour of her books, such as *Clearing in the West* and *The Black Creek Stopping House*.

Another ally is Louise McKinney (left), elected MLA for Claresholm in 1917. Henrietta Muir Edwards of Calgary (right) is an expert on legal matters.

Irene Parlby ensures the government's participation in the fight. Elected MLA for Alix in 1921, she becomes the second woman cabinet minister in the Empire. Here is Irene when she was a farm bride, with her dapper English husband Walter.

Murphy, McClung, McKinney, Edwards, and Parlby — the names of the Famous Five. With the full support of the government (and the advice of the attorney general), they carry the fight about whether women are people to the highest court in Canada and finally to London in 1929, where the Privy Council rules in their favour and in favour of all Canadian women. The Famous Five have the last word — wherever the word *person* appears in Canadian law, it applies equally.

The Alberta Provincial Police

FROM 1916 TO '33, a new generation of whisky traders operates along the Alberta-U.S. border. Prohibition is the cause, but there's some confusion about it. In 1916 Alberta puts in prohibition. In 1918 all the United States put it in. In 1923 Alberta takes it out, but the Americans keep trying until 1933. A big man will be needed to sort out the confusion.

This man looks big enough. He's William Brankley, veteran of a quarter-century with the Mounties. In 1917 Brankley is named commandant of the newly formed Alberta Provincial Police, a force which will replace the Mounties until 1932. When Brankley assumes command, Alberta bars are closed....

The bar of the Wainwright Hotel, seen here in Christmas trim. (The hotel is destined to burn down but to be rebuilt eventually as a feature of Heritage Park.)

At Jasper and 101st Street the Selkirk Hotel bar gleams empty, but bartender Jack Kearns has not suffered. He has gone to California to discover Jack Dempsey and will make him heavyweight boxing champion of the world.

Without its bar, the Strathcona Hotel knows a dry period as Westminster Ladies College.

Until the Alberta government gets into the liquor business, Brankley's men have a problem cartooned in the *Bob Edwards Summer Annual*.

But their heaviest duty is on the U.S. border. APP roadblocks are a familiar sight to motorists in the Crowsnest Pass. A very small barrier is sufficient to block the narrow gravel highway.

Roar of the Twenties (Roar of the Crowd)

JUST BEFORE HIS BAFFLING DISAPPEARANCE, Toronto show-business magnate Ambrose Small finances construction of his last theatre. Here is the New Empire in Edmonton, ready for opening night in 1920. A lavish production of the London musical *Maid of the Mountains* gives the New Empire an impressive start. But the day of the big theatre is already past. A later generation will recognize the stage as the bandstand of the Trocadero Ballroom.

Live theatre and vaudeville are losing out to moving pictures, which have exciting new personalities and inventive advertisers.

Taxidermist Frank Wolfe helps the Rialto announce the run of *God's Country and the Woman,* a story of Alberta's northern woods by James Oliver Curwood. Curwood's book was called *Back to God's Country.* Hollywood has added a further attraction.

In Calgary, Dad Leach alternates vaudeville with movies at popular prices — six cents for kids at the Saturday matinee.

In 1926 two Hollywood stunt planes land at RCAF Station High River. They're in Alberta to film a daredevil chase, flying across the face of the glacier at Lake Louise. The wings are being painted black and white to make them show up against the snowy background. The movie, logically, is called *Pyjamas*.

In 1928 the Palace Theatre proclaims the run of *His Destiny*, a Gaumont-British epic of the Wild West, partly filmed at the Calgary Stampede and partly on the ranch of Guy Weadick, the event's eminent founder.

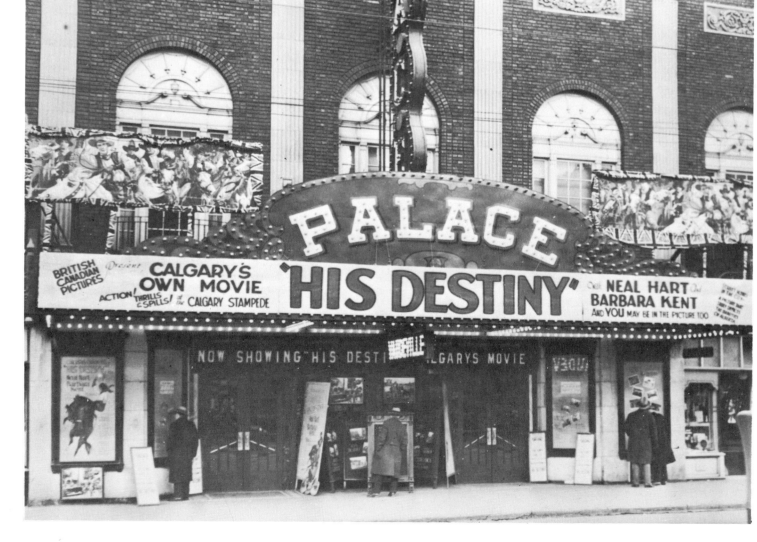

In 1920 a movie crew comes to Fort Macleod to film *Cameron of the Royal Mounted.* Residents of the nearby Blood Reserve have dressed up in Hollywood costumes and surrounded the train.

However, the Indians had better watch out. Here comes the hero, played by Gaston Glass. He's got them outnumbered one to fifty.

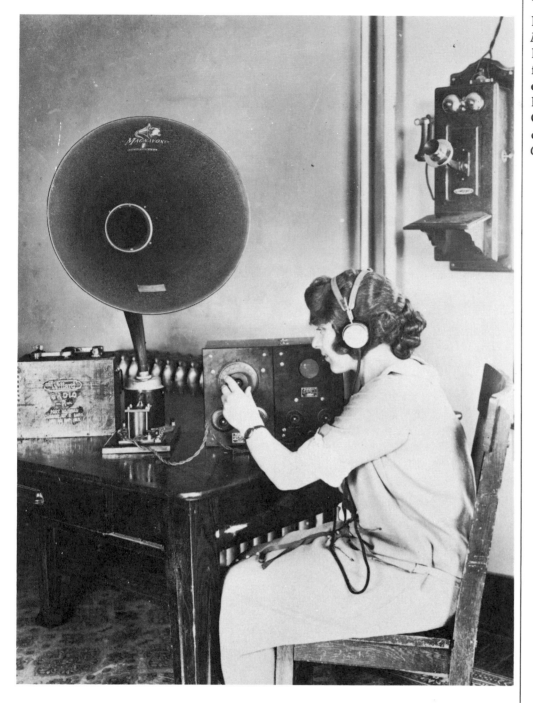

Epics like *Cameron of the Royal Mounted* lure people out of their homes and into movie theatres, but for the first time in history a mass entertainment medium makes house calls. Photographer B. S. Cameron of Ponoka titles this study of a young woman *The Radio Operator*.

In 1922 and '23 some four-letter combinations enter the consciousness of Alberta: CJCA, CFCN, CFAC — and CJOC, which entertains from this studio.

Wilf Carter, the yodelling cowboy, is a popular personality on CFCN.

So is this gentleman. In 1925 he begins broadcasting from the Prophetic Bible Institute.

Thanks to radio, no area is so remote as to miss out on the rhythm of the Roaring Twenties. Local bands keep up with the latest trends in popular music. The Whiz-Bang-Zowie Orchestra performs for dances around Byemoor.

This basketball squad is also moving in time to the beat of the twenties.

The Edmonton Commercial Grads are ahead of their time. In 1924 they leave for Paris and the Olympic Games.

"The Grads have the greatest basketball team that ever stepped out on a floor." One man's opinion, but the man is Doctor James Naismith, who invented basketball. The Grads win all their games in Paris, but there is no gold for Canada as women's basketball is not yet an official Olympic event.

The 1921 Eskimos are also off — to Toronto. Led by coach Deacon White, they're the first western team to challenge for the Grey Cup. Years later, fans of the Calgary Stampeders will make the Grey Cup national madness — but this team makes it national.

Do they win like the Grads? As a matter of fact, no. They lose to Toronto Varsity by 23-0. But the unkindest cut is suffered on ice. In 1926 owners of the *National* Hockey League want teams for New York, Boston, Detroit, and Chicago. They engineer the break-up of the Western Canada Professional League and stars like Duke Keats come no more to challenge the Calgary Tigers at Victoria Arena.

Road Show

HERE IS THE VERY PICTURE of changing times and a changing pace. It's the Sundre Stampede of 1924. Visitors have come from near and far. With the newest thing in transportation they've come farther than ever before. In the foreground are the buggies of spectators who have come by traditional transport. But, out beyond, is a crescent of automobiles.

Stunt driver Paul Welch publicizes automobiling the way barnstorming pilots push aviation. On a bet, he drives up the steepest slope on Calgary's Northeast Hill. In 1922, on another bet, he drives Edmonton to Calgary and return in just under ten hours, while many spectators remember when the journey took just under ten days.

By 1924 it's no longer necessary to drive to Banff in a convoy of Auto Club cars while a repair truck loaded with spare parts brings up the rear.

Alberta begins the decade with thirty-four thousand cars. By 1929 there are ninety-seven thousand, and the province is making a quarter of its income from the gasoline tax. However, no paved roads await the motorists. There's a clear need for auto laundries. Here is Calgary's first.

And if you have to go you may as well go in style with Connelly and McKinley in the first automotive hearse west of Toronto.

Alberta's growing appetite for oil is a boon to the wildcatters who keep prospecting for a local supply. At the end of the Alberta and Great Waterways railroad there's a known supply — if only a method can be found to separate it from the sand.

In March 1920, in a shack near Fort McMurray, Daniel Diver seeks a process. Diver is steaming oil from tar sand in the Rogers Golden Syrup can. With patience, eight pounds of sand will yield twelve ounces of crude oil.

In the mid-twenties Royalite, Home, and Okalta make discoveries at Turner Valley that maintain hope of big strikes elsewhere. In the still of the night W. J. Oliver photographs the Okalta derrick by the light of its own gas flare.

In 1929 all omens are favourable. The next year Alberta will gain control of the natural resources that have been held up to now by the national government.

A Calgary art firm is asked to design a cover for the magazine *Canada Illustrated* (published in England) and makes an amusing "improvement" on the provincial crest. The improved crest is set on a background of Number One Northern wheat, which the world is eager to buy at a dollar a bushel. The rectangles formed by the Cross of St. George, atop the crest, are usually wasted, but here we see four pictures of coal mining and agriculture — much better. At the foot of the great mountains, where the Marquis of Lorne drew "the yellow prairie stretching as far as the eye could see," the artist has placed several oil derricks, and in case the point should be missed, a gusher and an oil derrick have been placed in cameo like pillars supporting the crest.

In addition to an improved crest, Alberta gains a floral emblem, a roadside flower. The campaign is conducted by the Women's Institutes, which are very close to the UFA government. In 1929 the WIs invite the school children of the province to choose the flower that means Alberta. The tiger lily draws some support, but the clear winner is *Rosa acicularis,* the wild rose.

Applauding the choice, the Lethbridge *Herald* notes that it's a flower for all seasons: "The wild rose beautifies the summer landscape and its scarlet berries brighten the winter."

R.B. Bennett,
Prime Minister for Depression

IN 1930 THE ROSE-HUED HORIZONS have turned dark and stormy — and Calgary's R. B. Bennett achieves his ambition to be prime minister of Canada. He is greeted at the CPR station platform on his first trip home after the victory. Although the depression is closing its grip on the country, Bennett remains confident that he can "blast his way" into the markets of the world.

Dazzling orator, millionaire, industrialist, general counsel for the Canadian Pacific Railway, Bennett is at ease in top hat and striped trousers. He is clearly an uncommon man, and at this trying period in history he has no rapport with the common man, the fellow who is taking the worst beating.

The top hat and striped trousers are symbols of wealth and privilege. Bennett is a convenient target for cartoon and lampoon. He is powerless to influence the course of the depression, and in the next five years he becomes identified with all the symbols of that time: with hopping freights. . . .

. . . with dust storms like this black brute bearing down on Okotoks in 1933, with soup kitchens, with pick-and-shovel relief work. . . .

. . . with line-ups of farm wagons waiting for relief feed. This winter scene is not from a Russian film of a Tolstoy novel — it's Acadia Valley, Alberta.

R. B. Bennett even gets his name attached to a vehicle — a car that has been converted back to horse power. Most Bennett Buggies at least have four wheels, but Sinai Goddard of Redwater has a Roman-style chariot.

A symbol of Bennett public works is a retaining wall along the river in Calgary. Across the U.S. border, President Roosevelt can put armies to work throwing huge dams across the Columbia River at Bonneville and Grand Coulee. Canada is so much smaller, so much poorer, that the best Bennett can manage is a wall to protect the Centre Street Bridge from the Bow River.

Social Credit

DESPERATE TIMES SUGGEST desperate remedies. By 1935 the leader of the Canadian Communist Party receives a civic welcome in the coal town of Nordegg. But Alberta is turning to another solution, and in an age of concern about the forgotten man here's one who is truly forgotten.

He's Maurice Colebourne, on the right, filming a scene from *Arms and the Man* and embracing Angela Baddeley, renowned later in her career as Mrs. Bridges, the cook in "Upstairs Downstairs." Maurice Colebourne is an English traveller and a writer in addition to being an actor. He has written a book called *Unemployment or War*, which outlines the Social Credit economic theories of Major C. H. Douglas.

The book has been drawn to the attention of William Aberhart, principal of Crescent Heights High School in Calgary and well-known radio personality through his broadcasts from the Prophetic Bible Institute.

Aberhart is drawn into politics by his concern for graduating high-school students who have no jobs to go to. As election day approaches in 1935, youth is the theme of Social Credit's float in the Calgary Stampede.

At the Ogden railway shops his supporters have converted a CPR speeder into a float. On August 22nd Social Credit sweeps to power with fifty-six seats of the sixty-three-seat house, and Alberta's third political dynasty is founded. All trace of the second dynasty (the UFA) is swept away, even the premier. The Social Credit regime will last thirty-six years.

On the first anniversary of victory, enthusiasm runs high at a picnic on St. George's Island. Mr. Aberhart addresses the crowd while his successor, Ernest C. Manning, watches from the platform.

THE GOVERNMENT OF THE PROVINCE OF ALBERTA

PROSPERITY CERTIFICATE

DATE OF ISSUE
AUGUST 5, 1936   A   73091

THE PROVINCIAL TREASURER WILL PAY TO THE BEARER THE SUM OF ONE DOLLAR ON THE EXPIRATION OF TWO YEARS FROM DATE OF ISSUE HEREOF UPON PRESENTATION HEREOF PROVIDED THERE ARE THEN ATTACHED TO THE BACK HEREOF ONE HUNDRED AND FOUR ONE CENT CERTIFICATE STAMPS

ONE DOLLAR

William Aberhart
PREMIER

C. Cockcroft
PROVINCIAL TREASURER

WESTERN PRINTING & LITHOGRAPHING CO. LTD. CALGARY

The Aberhart government has introduced a form of currency with a message for the depression. A prosperity certificate has the face value of a dollar.

210

ALBERTA 1 CENT	ALBERTA 1 CENT	ALBERTA 1 CENT	ALBERTA 1 CENT	ALBERTA 1 CENT	ALBERTA 1 CENT	SEPT. 23, 1936	SEPT. 30, 1936	OCT. 7, 1936	OCT. 14, 1936	OCT. 21, 1936	OCT. 28, 1936	NOV. 4, 1936	NOV. 12, 1936	NOV. 18, 1936
NOV. 25, 1936	DEC. 2, 1936	DEC. 9, 1935	DEC. 16, 1936	DEC. 23, 1936	DEC. 30, 1936	JAN. 6, 1937	JAN. 13, 1937	JAN. 20, 1937	JAN. 27, 1937	FEB. 3, 1937	FEB. 10, 1937	FEB. 17, 1937	FEB. 24, 1937	MAR. 3, 1937
MAR. 10, 1937	MAR. 17, 1937	MAR. 24, 1937	MAR. 31, 1937	APRIL 7, 1937	APRIL 14, 1937	APRIL 21, 1937	APRIL 28, 1937	MAY 5, 1937	MAY 12, 1937	MAY 19, 1937	MAY 26, 1937	JUNE 2, 1937	JUNE 9, 1937	JUNE 16, 1937
JUNE 23, 1937	JUNE 30, 1937	JULY 7, 1937	JULY 14, 1937	JULY 21, 1937	JULY 28, 1937	AUG. 4, 1937	AUG. 11, 1937	AUG. 18, 1937	AUG. 25, 1937	SEPT. 1, 1937	SEPT. 8, 1937	SEPT. 15, 1937	SEPT. 22, 1937	SEPT. 29, 1937
OCT. 6, 1937	OCT. 13, 1937	OCT. 20, 1937	OCT. 27, 1937	NOV. 3, 1937	NOV. 10, 1937	NOV. 17, 1937	NOV. 24, 1937	DEC. 1, 1937	DEC. 8, 1937	DEC. 15, 1937	DEC. 22, 1937	DEC. 29, 1937	JAN. 5, 1938	JAN. 12, 1938
JAN. 19, 1938	JAN. 26, 1938	FEB. 2, 1938	FEB. 9, 1938	FEB. 16, 1938	FEB. 23, 1938	MAR. 2, 1938	MAR. 9, 1938	MAR. 16, 1938	MAR. 23, 1938	MAR. 30, 1938	APRIL 6, 1938	APRIL 13, 1938	APRIL 20, 1938	APRIL 27, 1938
MAY 4, 1938	MAY 11, 1938	MAY 18, 1938	MAY 25, 1938	JUNE 1, 1938	JUNE 8, 1938	JUNE 15, 1938	JUNE 22, 1938	JUNE 29, 1938	JULY 6, 1938	JULY 13, 1938	JULY 20, 1938	JULY 27, 1938	AUG. 3, 1938	

Each Monday for 104 weeks, the current holder is supposed to add a one-penny stamp, and at the end of two years the provincial treasurer will redeem it for $2.04. Most certificates, like this one, go out of circulation to be souvenirs.

The government of freshman legislators has much to learn. An important role in the learning process will be played by John Campbell Bowen, here signing the oath of lieutenant-governor on March 23rd, 1937. He is watched by Aberhart, Manning (to the left of the speaker), and Chief Justice Horace Harvey. The next two years will bring tense confrontations involving the government, the courts, and the lieutenant-governor exercising the constitutional power retained by the crown. Former harvest hand, Baptist minister, Edmonton city councillor, and leader of the provincial opposition, Bowen will be forced to a lonely stand, refusing royal assent to bills (which would send a critical newspaper reporter to jail and impose regulations on the banks) which the courts will rule are beyond the powers of a provincial government. A rough start for Alberta's sixth lieutenant-governor, but he will serve thirteen years, longer than any.

Beating the Depression

BEATING THE DEPRESSION is a game played by one or more persons. Players recognize that they can't actually beat the depression. The object of the game is to keep it from beating you — or a neighbour — until it eventually disappears. The first rule of the game asserts the transitory nature of the depression: It's gotta end sometime.

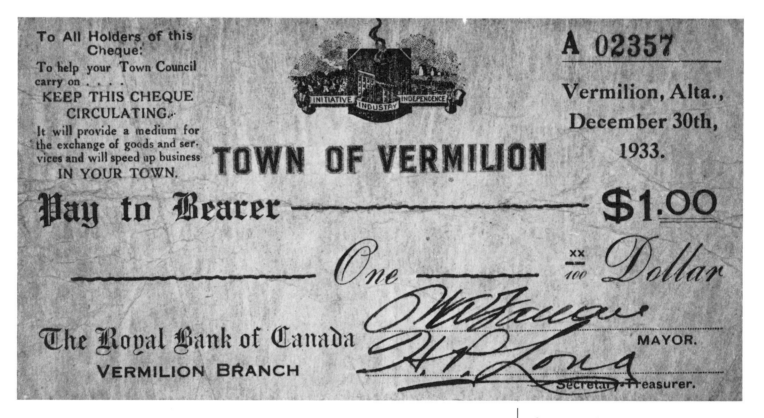

The town of Vermilion plays an interesting form of the game. To pay its municipal bills, the town issues paper currency with a face value of a dollar. Paper must be backed by something of course, and this is backed by the uncollectable taxes of those who own property or conduct business in Vermilion.

In 1938 this motto becomes the title of a popular magazine story, one of the publishing surprises of the year. Appearing in the *Saturday Evening Post*, it brings instant fame to the writer and to the Alberta farm family he has created. The writer is R. Ross Annett, principal of the school at Consort. The family are Big Joe, his orphaned children Babe and Little Joe, and rascally Uncle Pete who fights the depression by transforming lowly potato peels into whisky.

Although recognizably Albertan, Big Joe's family is accepted by six million readers of the *Saturday Evening Post* as typical of all farm families of the North American central plain, gamely waiting out the dust bowl. They are so popular that they appear in the *Post* seventy times and acquire images created by the author and Amos Sewell, a Connecticut artist who draws from photographs sent by the author.

Ross Annett is paid five hundred dollars for the first story, and in the dried-out town of Consort the coming of a cheque of such magnitude is one of the success stories people tell to help each other beat the depression.

IT'S GOTTA RAIN SOMETIME

"Another Good Blow of Wind From the Right Direction, or a Few Hours With a Shovel, and She'll be in the Clear"

"Pop!" cried eight-year-old Little Joe

Forty years later, a Mounted Policeman who served in Alberta throughout this time will read all the books about the thirties — which, incidentally, were not dirty — and complain that he never reads about anyone helping the less lucky person. But it's the most widespread version of the game. That person may appear anywhere, anytime, most often at the kitchen door, asking for a meal. These travellers will dine tonight, and tomorrow, and every night until the depression is over. It's gotta end sometime.

Optimism is not irrational. People seek reasons for it. Oil men keep up the hope for a major industry, with finds at Turner Valley, Lloydminster, and Wainwright. Meridian Number One, at Ribstone, proves a mild success for its backers, including Eric Harvie who draws attention to the trickle of oil. In years far ahead, Harvie's confidence in oil will fund the Glenbow-Alberta Institute and allied cultural efforts.

The tar sands remain a cause for optimism, though in the early thirties, when Alberta has forty miles of paved highway, the dominant thought is of pavement.

Reverting to a technique of the fur traders, these vigorous fellows are tracking barges of sand to the railroad at McMurray.

This load has arrived at Jasper Park where it will be used to pave the station platform, and millionaires getting off the train en route to the lodge will be sure to notice. It's clear that many millions are required to cash in on the promise of the tar sands. Exploiting the tar sands depends on an extraction process; so does beating the depression — you have to get the most out of whatever there is.

Beating the depression might involve afternoon cakes at the Tea Kettle Inn on Calgary's Seventh Avenue — in an atmosphere of hunting prints.

It might be a pile of automotive parts from which a gentleman of Endiang has achieved a working snowmobile.

Or it might be the Glenora Carnival. The economic conditions that have put young people on the road have taken big entertainment off. Ice shows won't come to a remote city of eighty thousand. These girls, along with other members of the Glenora Skating Club, are getting their act together for the carnival, a very big annual event in Edmonton, where one-hundred-dollar municipal bonds sell for sixty-five dollars. During carnival week, a quarter of the population will ride streetcars to the east-end arena to enjoy the show and the effort club members have put into it.

There is an elite band of adventurers who actually do beat the depression — and give lesser mortals the vicarious thrill of northland adventure and commercial success.

By the early thirties, development of the airplane has made it dependable for long flights over rough country. Here all the aircraft operating from the Edmonton Municipal Airport are grouped in front of the lone hangar. The biplanes belong to the Flying Club, which is turning out still more bush pilots. Since Leigh Brintnell is paying the photographer, he gets to put his Fairchild 71 up front.

There is no concrete on the field, even in front of the hangar. Winter is not a great problem — except around the edges. This northern freighter has tried to bounce off on wheels through the first snow and failed. Mechanics are putting on skis.

When flying far from home, a pilot has to do his own emergency work. Here is Matt Berry down on a nameless northern lake. The pontoon began flapping in midair. Matt has come down and secured it with a sturdy rope.

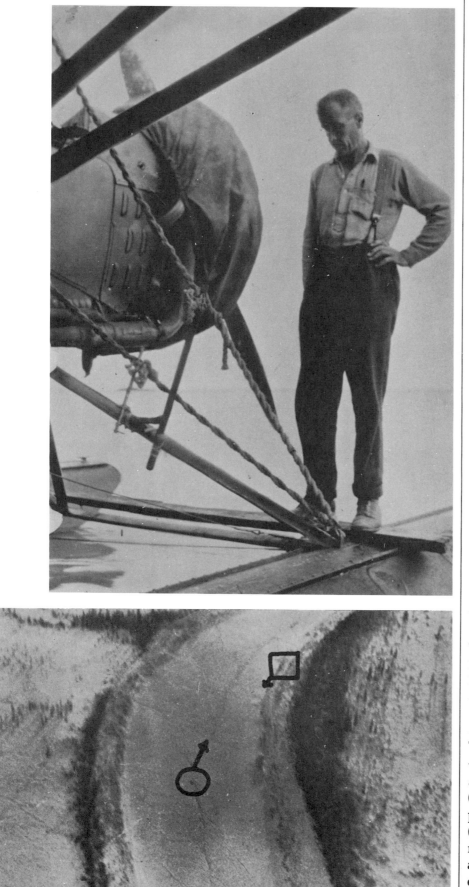

The names of the bush pilots are household words — Punch Dickins, Walter Gilbert, Harry Hayter, Jack Moar, Gil McLaren, Marlowe Kennedy, Archie McMullen. They are involved in all the dramas of the north — mercy flights and the hunt for the Mad Trapper of Red River. The last gun battle of the Trapper is witnessed from the air by Wop May and Jack Bowen. The Trapper (circle) has just turned and sees the pursuing Mounted Policemen (square). This picture will appear in newspapers all over North America and will be scanned avidly by readers who have been following the drama for days.

There are cargoes beyond the roads and railroads that make air transport economically viable, even in the grind of depression. Gold is one. Wop May picks up freight and passengers at Goldfields in 1933.

In a blizzard at Fort McMurray, concentrated ore is loaded aboard a plane for the flight south.

There are no landing fields in the north. The bush pilots use lakes and rivers, attaching skis in the winter and floats in the summer. This is Grant McConachie's first Ford tri-motor, known as the "Tin Goose." On contract from fish broker Bill Schlader, the future organizer and president of Canadian Pacific Airlines gets a start flying fish from Buffalo Lake to Edmonton for the big fish markets of Chicago.

Yellowknife gold is discovered by aerial exploration. Gilbert Labine flies to discover uranium at Eldorado on Great Bear Lake. On Dominion Day 1933 Gilbert invites all the bush pilots to a party at Eldorado, and to make it a success he flies in eighty cases of party favours. All the legends are here. That's Stan McMillan on the right, with Con Farrell in plus fours. Depression? Not here.

World War II

By 1939 THE CLOUDS of depression are breaking. But clouds more ominous are gathering — those of war. In the summer, King George VI and Queen Elizabeth make a royal procession across Canada to rally the tired country for another ordeal. People who have endured one world war and the depression will have to watch sons and daughters go off to another conflict about which there are no illusions.

George VI is the first reigning monarch to visit Alberta. The excitement is captured by Wainwright's veteran photographer, J. H. Gano. Long before the train is expected, the station yard is jammed by people who have come from a hundred miles north and south of the railroad line.

At last the special train pulls in, and the crowds push forward — for a glimpse of the royal party on the platform.

In September the war comes.

EXTRA

If You Don't Get The Bulletin, You Don't Get All the News Nor the Pictures

THE WEATHER

GOVERNMENT WEATHER FORECAST
Today and Friday—Fair and warm.
Sun rises Friday 5:43. Sets 7:24. Light vehicles by 7:44.
Edmonton temperatures—Noon yesterday to 9 a.m. today: Maximum, 71 above; Minimum, 40 above.

Edmonton Bulletin
AN INDEPENDENT NEWSPAPER IN PUBLIC SERVICE

FIFTY-NINTH YEAR. VOL. LIX, No. 204

EDMONTON, ALBERTA—FRIDAY, SEPTEMBER 1, 1939

WHEAT CLOSE

THURSDAY
WINNIPEG CLOSING — Oct. 59; Nov. 60½; Dec. 60½; May, 63½.

Single Copy, Five Cents

WAR

POLAND IS INVADED BY NAZI ARMS

Amid shattering blasts of heavy artillery and the crash of aerial bombardments, war broke out along the Polish-German frontier at about 9:55 p.m. Thursday night. German

EUROPE'S NAVAL TONNAGE
Great Britain ...... 2,100,000 tons
France .... 800,000 tons
Total .... 2,900,000 tons
Italy ..... 700,000 tons
Germany ... 550,000 tons
Total .... 1,250,000 tons

DANZIG IS IN HANDS OF HITLER

WARSAW, Sept. 1.—Poland, it was stated here last night, will insist on full restitution of her rights in Danzig.

BERLIN, Sept. 1.—Fuehrer Hitler today accepted the free city of Danzig into the reich. The fuehrer acted after Albert Forster, Nazi chief of state of the free city and Nazi district leader there, had proclaimed the reunion of the Baltic city with Hitler's Germany, and begged the Fuehrer to accept it.

War spreads around the world, its every action and emotion recorded by clicking, grinding cameras. But in Alberta the camera sees only young people on the move. They move by trains, on and off station platforms, in an endless parade of khaki and two shades of blue. The railroad station is the stage for wartime drama.

Recruits for the Canadian army, just out of high school, wait for the train at Edson.

In May 1940 the Calgary Highlanders depart for besieged Britain. The faces of the soldiers have blurred slightly as the train begins to move.

In October the same station sees the arrival of airmen from Australia and New Zealand. The first wave of air crews from "down under" come to flying fields in Alberta for the British Commonwealth Air Training Plan. They're delighted to find the first snow of winter falling. They're looking forward to learning to skate — supported by Canadian girls.

There are some fifteen air bases in the province. At the Edmonton Municipal Airport young women refuel an Anson navigation trainer. Three thousand airmen from the Commonwealth and allied nations will pass through this one school.

By 1942 the conflict has spread to the Pacific and the skies of Alberta become a funnel for American planes carrying the war to Japan. People look up to see squadrons of fighters, medium bombers, and this C-54 Skymaster transport, the largest aircraft ever seen over Edmonton. The skyline has not changed at all since the First World War, and though the streets look quiet, people are busy again.

Some young Americans on the move are ferrying warplanes to Russia. Others have come to build a highway and an oil pipeline to Alaska. In 1941 it was beyond imagining that a U.S. Army dance band could be at Fort Smith, just across the northern boundary of Alberta, playing Count Basie's arrangement of "Jumpin' at the Woodside." But it's 1943, and here they are.

The sounds of big-band music are the universal language of youth. This is a dance at the YMCA in Calgary.

Some of the dancers wear uniforms of the navy, the sign of a strong interest among prairie lads in service at sea — a surprise to navy psychologists, until they note a parallel between the great lonely spaces of prairie and ocean.

But for one body of soldiers who come to Alberta, there are no dances. These are the German prisoners of war who go behind barbed wire — like this fence near Medicine Hat.

The war goes on for almost five years. Finally, on June 6th, 1944, the cause comes to a crucial hour. At dawn the Allies land in France. That afternoon in Calgary, an impromptu outdoor service brings a solemn crowd to First Street Southeast.

Another year and it's over. And the CPR station, witness to so many personal dramas of separation, sets a stage for the closing scenes of World War II.

The Big Time

As THERE WAS NO returning to happy-go-lucky prewar 1914, so there is no going back to dreary prewar 1939. Victory releases a surge of assurance that something will turn up, something to employ the young people coming home from war. It's only a feeling, not shared by the older generation or the top economic experts among them.

Air force veteran Max Ward typifies the spirit of '46. This Fox Moth biplane on the water at Yellowknife is the entire fleet of what will become Wardair, the biggest charter airline in Canada, based in Alberta.

Wardair '46 can transport three passengers three hundred and fifty miles at eighty-five miles per hour. In times to come, Wardair will have fourteen jetliners to transport three thousand passengers five thousand miles at five hundred miles per hour.

In 1946 a cherished holiday is a trip to the coast — by train. In times to come, a filing clerk on her first vacation will fly to the coast of Oahu or Mexico or Spain.

Something very big is going to happen.

Here it is. After 133 consecutive failures, on February 13th, 1947, Imperial Oil is pleased to announce the arrival of Imperial Leduc Number One, the discovery of the Leduc field and the signal for many important finds to follow.

After decades of feeling second rate, Alberta regains the confidence of its youth. Reassurance bursts forth in many places. In Calgary's Victoria Arena, hockey fans raise the ancient roof, cheering on the Stampeders to the Allan Cup, symbol of supremacy in senior amateur hockey and a prize for which all Canadian cities compete in regional and national playoffs.

In 1946, for the first time, the Calgary Stampeders bring the Allan Cup to Alberta. In 1948 it's the turn of the Edmonton Flyers. Then, in November 1948, four hundred Calgarians accompany the football Stampeders to Toronto to help their team challenge for the Grey Cup. And in one high-spirited, spontaneous weekend a Canadian national tradition is born.

Here comes the very first Grey Cup parade. Led by Toronto's mayor Hiram ("Buck") McCallum, on a dark horse, truck-loads of Stampeder fans parade from the Royal York Hotel to Varsity Stadium while curious residents of Toronto watch in astonishment.

The outcome is history. The scoreboard reads: Calgary 12, Ottawa 7. Headlines read: Western Parade Thrills East. Civic Holiday on Stamps' Return.

The next season, Edmonton puts a team in the league. The programme reflects the sudden significance of oil derricks, and the goal posts are still in the shape of an H. That's appropriate because the H can stand for Hope — and that's about all Alberta has, since no one has yet seen much actual oil money.

The green and gold uniforms are hand-me-downs from the University of Alberta, which has given up football. Games are played Saturday night so as not to crimp Saturday afternoon sales at the department stores — they're contributing one thousand dollars each to the team.

The city contributes a four-thousand seat grandstand built with heavy timbers salvaged from an old bridge across Groat Ravine. The simple wooden grandstand is on the scale of everything in Alberta, as a forty-two-thousand-seat stadium built for the Commonwealth Games will be on the scale of 1978.

In the era just beginning, every activity in the province will expand and magnify to dimensions undreamed of. The Citadel Theatre complex is beyond the imagining of fans listening to the Eskimos' sideline announcer in 1949, but the Citadel will be founded by the announcer, a recent law graduate named Joe Schoctor.

And one of the players to whom Joe draws attention from time to time has a future on a big scale.

FOOTBALL PROGRAM

PETE LOUGHEED

Age, 21 years; weight, 158 lbs.; height, 5'7"; born at Calgary.

Schools: Calgary Central High, University of Alberta.

Football Experience

Five years Calgary Junior Tornadoes; 2 years Alberta Golden Bears.

Position—Halfback.

Other Sports—Hockey and Track.

Single.

He stands five-foot-seven, weighs 158 pounds, and plays professional football — Peter Lougheed obviously packs a lot of determination. In 1971 he will lead the Conservative party into office and end the Social Credit dynasty after thirty-six years.

As premier he will preside at the birth of the Syncrude project — a project physically, technically, and financially beyond the comprehensions of 1949.

An aerial view taken in October 1977 conveys only the physical dimensions. Those toylike trucks and bulldozers are full-size, dwarfed by the giant dragline that is digging out the McMurray oil sands. The dragline has a boom 110 yards long — appropriately the length of a football field.

As Alberta builds toward Syncrude, 1955 brings the province to a moment of historical perspective. As the sign on the lamppost says: Calgary Salutes Alberta's Golden Years. A parade is approaching, and first place goes to citizens who remember the events of that inaugural September.

The government's big anniversary present is matching Jubilee Auditoriums for Calgary and Edmonton. Concert artists coming to Edmonton will no longer have to compete with aromas of livestock in the exhibition grounds' sales pavilion or the sounds of passing trains. The only artist to compete successfully with the trains has been Viennese soprano Erna Sack, who paused in mid-song to trill in tune with the engine whistles.

These scenes could be either Calgary or Edmonton. In the lobbies, in the concert halls, the Golden Jubilee auditoriums offer a major league environment for the enjoyment and performance of great music.

Alberta can afford the best. Beverly Sills is the greatest in her field. On her fourth appearance with the Edmonton Opera Association, she accepts applause for her *Daughter of the Regiment*.

While quaint ways make a last stand here and there, history sweeps on. In 1958 the camera is called on to record a symbolic comeback — the first appointment of a native Canadian to the Senate. James Gladstone, of the Blood tribe of southern Alberta, poses for an official portrait.

His elevation to the Senate comes exactly fifty years after promoters of the Calgary Dominion Exhibition urged the curious to "hurry, hurry, hurry — the cowboys and Indians will soon be gone."

In ages past the Indian had a mobile home. Now, changing work and leisure patterns are making the mobile popular again — the trailer on wheels and the home that can be moved. Eventually, the mobile home park becomes a feature of every community, like Westview Village at Spruce Grove.

As the mobile home casts its geometry on townsites, the suburban shopping centre begins to reshape the commercial and traffic patterns of the cities. This is the first of them, Westmount Shoppers Park, shortly after its opening in 1954. Coronation Park, beyond, is still in its agricultural state. Rounded cars, seeking entrance to the parking lot, try to master that new phenomenon in traffic flow, the traffic circle.

In the surge toward new dimensions, the laws governing alcohol remain firmly entrenched in a simple past. Breweries produce ginger ale so that they can rent billboards and make coy allusions to their beer. An American journalist, come to report on the oil boom, writes with sly humour that Albertans seem madly addicted to ginger ale. Liquor and wine are sold only in government stores, with the purchaser signing for each item. In country taverns men and women may call for beer together, but in the cities they consume in separate rooms.

Through the fifties, the cities spread outward. In the next decade they begin to reach upward. In 1963 a strange shape takes form on the ruins of Calgary's sandstone CPR station.

It's the launching pad for a concrete shaft soaring more than five hundred feet into the sky, a shape that will identify Calgary as the Eiffel Tower identifies Paris.

The shape is the Calgary Tower, framed here by cranes making a further addition to the skyline. These machines are raising Gulf Canada Square, said to be the most energy-efficient building complex in Canada, one which consumes fossil fuel with heat from solar energy and recycles building heat through a hot-water system.

The crane, it's said, is the civic bird of Calgary. Lifted by the crane, the city's profile climbs skyward in a line of towers, many of them head-office towers with richly appointed boardrooms dedicated to talk of finance and oil exploration. Even the sidewalks rise fifteen feet in a programme to link downtown buildings with glassed-in elevated walk-ways. The Devonian Gardens offers a park with year-round summer climate, two and three storeys above Eighth Avenue.

The crane transforms the skyline of Edmonton too, as shown by this aerial view taken from the same point as the picture of 1942. Edmonton's profile goes many flights up and one flight down — down to the stations of the first subway system in western Canada. A rapid-transit train emerges from its tunnel, with downtown towers in the background.

On August 3rd, 1978, this picture is beamed around the world by TV satellite. Forty-two thousand people in the new Commonwealth Stadium — built within budget and in time — await the arrival of Diane Jones-Konihowski bearing the royal proclamation which the Queen will read to open the Commonwealth Games.

In the "big time" there occurs yet another important development: an interest in history. A discovery is made. Alberta has more than a past. It has a history worth telling in prose — and in pictures — a history worth incorporating into architecture. Here it gives distinctive character to the inaugural building of the University of Lethbridge. The campus is high on the rounding bluffs which the founders of the city called the coalbanks. A conventional building site would be the level ground on top. Instead, designer Arthur Erickson has set the building into a coulee, recalling the eighteen wooden trestles on which the rail-roaders brought the steel from Fort Macleod.

The interest in history is noted — and promoted — with the appointment of Alberta's ninth lieutenant-governor. Although Grant MacEwan is a man of several well-exercised talents in agriculture, education, physical fitness, and politics, provincial and civic (leader of the opposition and mayor of Calgary), he is known most widely for his books on western history.

His term of office (1965-74) is an extended lecture tour, bringing to life the people who fill his own writings and the preceding pages of this book.

Here he is being piped into St. Stanislaus School, Edmonton, where he will talk to the kids about "the olden days." It's a short parade for Grant MacEwan, who is normally seen leading thousands on

Marches for Millions. But it is symbolic. The kids represent the continuation of all that he's come to talk about — even the boy who plans to be a music critic when he grows up and makes his own mark on Alberta history.

Credits

This book is an expression of many things, including the public spirit of Eric Harvie, who translated good fortune with Alberta oil into cultural treasures. Three-quarters of the pictures came from the Glenbow-Alberta Institute in Calgary, founded and funded by Eric Harvie. The Glenbow photo archives are a *concentration* of riches so compact and so accessible that one may actually browse. The Harvie vision was broad; the Glenbow is a national institution. On any day one can find researchers from other parts of Canada trying to "get a handle" on subjects from Victorian techniques of sheep dipping to Edwardian attitudes toward the family. The friendly staff are there on a "May I help you?" basis. Sheilagh Jameson. Georgeen Barrass. Hugh Dempsey. They are all willing to help, and so able. There are resources at other institutions in Alberta but with any historical project the Glenbow is the place to start.

The sources of the non-Glenbow pictures are as follows:

Alberta Government Telephones, 75 (right), 76 (upper)
Art Carlyle, 210 (upper), 211 (upper)
Calgary Office of Business Development, 208 (lower)
City of Edmonton Archives, 134 (lower), 184, 185, 186, 187, 189 (lower), 191 (lower)
Edmonton Journal, 22 Michael Dean, 211 Brian J. Gavriloff (lower), 213
Edmonton Opera Association, 205 Michael Vann
Edmonton Transit System, 210 (lower)
Medicine Hat Pioneer Museum, cover photograph, 64 (upper), 102 (lower right), 113 (lower)
Mike's News Stand, 192 (upper)
National Film Archive, London, England (EMI), 175
Northern Alberta Jubilee Auditorium, 204

Provincial Archives of Alberta, 180; Ernest Brown Collection, 41 (lower), 65, 66 (upper), 67 (upper), 68, 69 (upper), 79 (upper), 98 (upper), 145; Harry Pollard Collection, 36 (lower), 40, 105 (lower left), 197
Public Archives of Canada, 33, 36 (upper)
RCMP Museum, Regina, 44 (lower), 61 (upper)
Royal Ontario Museum, 10, 11, 12
St. Albert Historical Society, 19 (lower)
TransCanada Pipelines, 46
University of Lethbridge, 212

Ruth Bowen, 178, 199
Tony Cashman (author's collection), 17 (upper), 20 (upper right), 49 (upper left), 200, 201
Gary Larue (Institute of Applied Art), 41 (upper), 49 (upper right)
Nelson MacDonald, 209 (lower)
Ken Orr, 202
Ranson, Edmonton, 13, 206 (lower), 207 (upper)
Ranson and Nodwell, Calgary, 209 (upper)
Monte Stout, 174 (lower)
F. A. Talbot, 71 (lower)
William Tidball, 165 (lower)
Vivian Thierfelder, sketch, 170 (lower)
Max Ward, 196

The untitled pictures on the introductory pages are all from the Glenbow. They are as follows:

Wop May drops a baseball from a plane to open the season of 1919 at Diamond Park, Edmonton.
Elbow Valley School.
Start of the *Edmonton Journal* boys' bicycle race, 1913.
Railroad building near Munson, 1909.
Homesteaders waiting for the land guide, near Vermilion, 1907.